Oracle Data Dictionary
Pocket Reference

David C. Kreines

Beijing · Cambridge · Farnham · Köln · Paris · Sebastopol · Taipei · Tokyo

Oracle Data Dictionary Pocket Reference
by David C. Kreines

Copyright © 2003 O'Reilly & Associates, Inc. All rights reserved.
Printed in the United States of America.

Published by O'Reilly & Associates, Inc., 1005 Gravenstein Highway North,
Sebastopol, CA 95472.

O'Reilly & Associates books may be purchased for educational,
business, or sales promotional use. Online editions are also available
for most titles (*safari.oreilly.com*). For more information, contact our
corporate/institutional sales department: (800) 998-9938 or
corporate@oreilly.com.

Editor:	Deborah Russell
Production Editor:	Sarah Sherman
Cover Designer:	Emma Colby
Interior Designer:	David Futato

Printing History:

April 2003:   First Edition

Nutshell Handbook, the Nutshell Handbook logo, and the O'Reilly
logo are registered trademarks of O'Reilly & Associates, Inc. Many of
the designations used by manufacturers and sellers to distinguish their
products are claimed as trademarks. Where those designations appear
in this book, and O'Reilly & Associates, Inc. was aware of a trademark
claim, the designations have been printed in caps or initial caps. Oracle®
and all Oracle-based trademarks and logos are trademarks or registered
trademarks of Oracle Corporation, Inc. in the United States and other
countries. O'Reilly & Associates, Inc. is independent of Oracle
Corporation. Java and all Java-based trademarks and logos are
trademarks or registered trademarks of Sun Microsystems, Inc. in the
United States and other countries. O'Reilly & Associates, Inc. is
independent of Sun Microsystems, Inc. The association between the
image of the tsetse fly and the topic of the Oracle data dictionary is a
trademark of O'Reilly & Associates, Inc.

While every precaution has been taken in the preparation of this book,
the publisher and author assume no responsibility for errors or
omissions, or for damages resulting from the use of the information
contained herein.

0-596-00517-2
[C]

Contents

Oracle Data Dictionary Pocket Reference

Introduction

The *Oracle Data Dictionary Pocket Reference* is a quick reference guide to the Oracle data dictionary. This guide pulls together information on the tables and views most commonly used by Oracle database administrators and developers, along with column specification listings and usage and performance tips. Given the small size of this pocket reference, this book obviously cannot serve as a complete reference to the use of the Oracle data dictionary. For more detailed information, refer to the Oracle documentation for your release. This book reflects the data dictionary contents as of Oracle9*i* Release 2.

Acknowledgments

Many thanks to those who helped in the preparation of this book. In particular, thanks to Jonathan Gennick who provided a technical review of the draft. I also appreciate all the good work of the O'Reilly crew in editing and producing this book. And, of course, thanks to Debby Russell for keeping this book on the fast track.

Conventions

UPPERCASE
   Indicates a SQL keyword when used in a query.

lowercase

> Indicates a table, view, or column name in a query. (In query results, Oracle displays columns in uppercase.)

Italic

> Indicates user-defined items such as filenames.

`Constant width`

> Indicates code examples and output.

\# When used in a column listing, indicates that the column has a NOT NULL constraint (which means the column cannot contain a NULL value). Because of space constraints (many column names are very long), we have omitted the NOT NULL display from the column listings. For example, in the TABLESPACES view, the column BLOCK_SIZE has a NOT NULL constraint associated with it and thus is displayed as:

```
BLOCK_SIZE                    #NUMBER
```

What Is the Data Dictionary?

The Oracle data dictionary is a collection of tables and related views that enable you to see the inner workings and structure of the Oracle database. By querying these tables and views, you can obtain information about every object and every user of the database. All of the Oracle monitoring tools look at the information available in the data dictionary and present it in an easy-to-use format.

Traditionally, the data dictionary has consisted of a series of views owned by the SYS user. These views, known as *static data dictionary views*, present information contained in tables that are updated when Oracle processes a Data Definition Language (DDL) statement. The SYS tables and views, as well as a set of public synonyms for the views, are created by the *catalog.sql* script. In addition, the installation of some Oracle features creates tables and views in the SYSTEM schema. In general, tables and views owned by SYSTEM exist to support functionality provided by PL/SQL stored procedures rather than fundamental Oracle functionality.

There is a second set of views known as *dynamic data dictionary views* or *dynamic performance views*, and commonly referred to as *V$ views*. These V$ views are based on a set of internal memory structures maintained by Oracle as virtual tables (which all begin with an "X$" prefix). Just as the static data dictionary views provide information about the database, the V$ views (and underlying X$ tables) provide information about the active instance.

Sample Queries in This Book

In describing many of the data dictionary views in this book, I've included examples of sample SQL queries that you might issue to examine or use the view. Because this code is provided only to illustrate a concept or technique, I haven't taken pains to provide queries that will return output that is easily readable or neatly formatted. For example, I've included the following query with the description of V$SYSTEM_PARAMETER:

```
SELECT name,value
FROM v$system_parameter
WHERE isdefault = 'FALSE';
```

In reality, because name is defined as VARCHAR2(64) and value is defined as VARCHAR2(512), an experienced SQL programmer might instead write this query as:

```
SELECT substr(name,1,33),substr(value,1,45)
FROM v$system_parameter
WHERE isdefault = 'FALSE';
```

or alternatively might use the COLUMN command from SQL*Plus as follows:

```
COLUMN name FORMAT A33
COLUMN value FORMAT A45
SELECT name, value
FROM v$system_parameter
WHERE isdefault = 'FALSE';
```

In this case, the query would return a line of 80 characters per row, which would be short enough to be readable on the screen. Of course, some of the information might be truncated if it is longer than the substrings defined! In any event, these short examples are simply intended to show general usage. You may need to adjust them slightly for your situation.

Static Data Dictionary Views

While new views are added with every version of Oracle, the static data dictionary views have existed in their current format since Oracle Version 6. These views, which are owned by SYS and built upon tables owned by SYS, provide the ability to access information about database objects.

Categories of Views

Most of the static data dictionary is constructed in a matrix fashion. The first way to categorize data dictionary views is by the breadth of information they cover. Views can be divided into three groups:

USER_ views
> Views that allow you to see objects you own. These view names begin with USER_, as in USER_TABLES and USER_INDEXES.

ALL_ views
> Views that allow you to see objects that you own or that you have been granted privileges to access. These view names begin with ALL_, as in ALL_TABLES and ALL_INDEXES.

DBA_ views
> Views that allow you to see all objects in the database, regardless of who owns them. Primarily, these views are for use by the DBA, and they begin with DBA_, as in DBA_TABLES and DBA_INDEXES.

There are also a handful of other views that provide information of general interest about the database.

The ALL_ views have the same structure as the DBA_ views. The USER_ views have the same structure as the DBA_ views except that they do not include the OWNER column. The views that exist in multiple forms (i.e., ALL_, DBA_, USER_) are listed in this book in the form *_viewname. So, for example, there are three *_TABLES views:

    ALL_TABLES
    DBA_TABLES
    USER_TABLES

In the following sections, I'll note when a particular view does not support all three varieties. Some views have only one form or do not follow this naming pattern, and those are listed without the wildcard character (*). Examples include DBA_IND_EXPRESSIONS and DICT_COLUMNS.

The second way to categorize data dictionary views is by content. Many of the USER_, ALL_, and DBA_ views are grouped in families, or functional categories, often according to how their view names end (e.g., TABLES, COLUMNS, and so on). Groups of views provide information about particular Oracle topics. Because related views in a particular category are sometimes used together, I've grouped them in the following way:

    Change Data Capture
    Constraints
    Data dictionary
    Indexes
    Jobs and Advanced Queuing
    Locks
    Log groups
    Materialized views
    Networking and distributed transactions
    Objects Option
    Partitioning

Programming and PL/SQL
Replication
Security and auditing
Server information
SQLJ
Storage
Tables, columns, and views

Within each category, views are listed alphabetically.

NOTE

If you cannot immediately find a particular data dictionary view you are searching for, check for the name in the book's index.

Commonly Used Static Data Dictionary Views

The following sections summarize the purpose and columns available in most of Oracle's static data dictionary views. There are more static views than can possibly fit in this compact book, so I've included those most commonly used by DBAs and developers. Many views are rather obscure and rarely used; I'm confident that you will find all of the views you are likely to actually use in these pages.

Change Data Capture

Oracle9i introduces a feature known as Change Data Capture, used primarily in data warehouses, which allows a user to create a set of change tables that can be used to publish changes to a set of underlying tables:

*_SOURCE_TAB_COLUMNS

Lists the columns in the source tables that are contained in change tables.

SOURCE_SCHEMA_NAME	#VARCHAR2(30)
SOURCE_TABLE_NAME	#VARCHAR2(30)
COLUMN_NAME	#VARCHAR2(30)

DATA_TYPE	VARCHAR2(106)
DATA_LENGTH	#NUMBER
DATA_PRECISION	NUMBER
DATA_SCALE	NUMBER
NULLABLE	VARCHAR2(1)

*_SOURCE_TABLES

Lists the links between change tables and their source tables.

| SOURCE_SCHEMA_NAME | #VARCHAR2(30) |
| SOURCE_TABLE_NAME | #VARCHAR2(30) |

*_SUBSCRIBED_COLUMNS

Lists the columns of published tables that have been subscribed to.

HANDLE	#NUMBER
SOURCE_SCHEMA_NAME	#VARCHAR2(30)
SOURCE_TABLE_NAME	#VARCHAR2(30)
COLUMN_NAME	#VARCHAR2(30)

*_SUBSCRIBED_TABLES

Lists all published tables that have been subscribed to.

HANDLE	#NUMBER
SOURCE_SCHEMA_NAME	#VARCHAR2(30)
SOURCE_TABLE_NAME	#VARCHAR2(30)
VIEW_NAME	VARCHAR2(30)
CHANGE_SET_NAME	#VARCHAR2(30)

*_SUBSCRIPTIONS

Lists all subscriptions.

HANDLE	#NUMBER
SET_NAME	#VARCHAR2(30)
USERNAME	#VARCHAR2(30)
CREATED	#DATE
STATUS	#VARCHAR2(1)
EARLIEST_SCN	#NUMBER
LATEST_SCN	#NUMBER
DESCRIPTION	VARCHAR2(30)
LAST_PURGED	DATE
LAST_EXTENDED	DATE

Constraints

The following views provide information about constraints and the columns included in the constraints:

*_CONS_COLUMNS

Shows which columns are affected by each constraint.

OWNER	#VARCHAR2(30)
CONSTRAINT_NAME	#VARCHAR2(30)
TABLE_NAME	#VARCHAR2(30)
COLUMN_NAME	VARCHAR2(4000)
POSITION	NUMBER

*_CONSTRAINTS

Lists all constraints defined in the database.

OWNER	#VARCHAR2(30)
CONSTRAINT_NAME	#VARCHAR2(30)
CONSTRAINT_TYPE	VARCHAR2(1)
TABLE_NAME	#VARCHAR2(30)
SEARCH_CONDITION	LONG
R_OWNER	VARCHAR2(30)
R_CONSTRAINT_NAME	VARCHAR2(30)
DELETE_RULE	VARCHAR2(9)
STATUS	VARCHAR2(8)
DEFERRABLE	VARCHAR2(14)
DEFERRED	VARCHAR2(9)
VALIDATED	VARCHAR2(13)
GENERATED	VARCHAR2(14)
BAD	VARCHAR2(3)
RELY	VARCHAR2(4)
LAST_CHANGE	DATE
INDEX_OWNER	VARCHAR2(30)
INDEX_NAME	VARCHAR2(30)
INVALID	VARCHAR2(7)
VIEW_RELATED	VARCHAR2(14)

Data dictionary

The following views provide information about the objects in the Oracle data dictionary:

*_CATALOG

Lists all tables, views, sequences, and synonyms in the database.

OWNER	#VARCHAR2(30)
TABLE_NAME	#VARCHAR2(30)
TABLE_TYPE	VARCHAR2(11)

*_DEPENDENCIES

Lists dependencies between database objects. Used to determine which objects become invalid after other objects are altered or dropped.

OWNER	#VARCHAR2(30)
NAME	#VARCHAR2(30)
TYPE	VARCHAR2(17)
REFERENCED_OWNER	VARCHAR2(30)

REFERENCED_NAME	VARCHAR2(64)
REFERENCED_TYPE	VARCHAR2(17)
REFERENCED_LINK_NAME	VARCHAR2(128)
DEPENDENCY_TYPE	VARCHAR2(4)

DICT_COLUMNS

Lists all columns defined in the data dictionary views.

TABLE_NAME	VARCHAR2(30)
COLUMN_NAME	VARCHAR2(30)
COMMENTS	VARCHAR2(4000)

DICTIONARY

Lists all data dictionary views.

| TABLE_NAME | VARCHAR2(30) |
| COMMENTS | VARCHAR2(4000) |

*_OBJECTS

Lists all objects in the database. Note that this name predates the Oracle Objects Option and is not restricted to objects created using the Objects Option.

OWNER	VARCHAR2(30)
OBJECT_NAME	VARCHAR2(128)
SUBOBJECT_NAME	VARCHAR2(30)
OBJECT_ID	NUMBER
DATA_OBJECT_ID	NUMBER
OBJECT_TYPE	VARCHAR2(18)
CREATED	DATE
LAST_DDL_TIME	DATE
TIMESTAMP	VARCHAR2(19)
STATUS	VARCHAR2(7)
TEMPORARY	VARCHAR2(1)
GENERATED	VARCHAR2(1)
SECONDARY	VARCHAR2(1)

Indexes

The following views provide information about indexes and indexed columns:

DBA_IND_EXPRESSIONS

Lists all indexed expressions.

INDEX_OWNER	#VARCHAR2(30)
INDEX_NAME	#VARCHAR2(30)
TABLE_OWNER	#VARCHAR2(30)
TABLE_NAME	#VARCHAR2(30)
COLUMN_EXPRESSION	LONG
COLUMN_POSITION	#NUMBER

*_IND_COLUMNS

Lists all indexed columns.

INDEX_OWNER	#VARCHAR2(30)
INDEX_NAME	#VARCHAR2(30)
TABLE_OWNER	#VARCHAR2(30)
TABLE_NAME	#VARCHAR2(30)
COLUMN_NAME	VARCHAR2(4000)
COLUMN_POSITION	#NUMBER
COLUMN_LENGTH	#NUMBER
CHAR_LENGTH	NUMBER
DESCEND	VARCHAR2(4)

NOTE

You can use the *_IND_COLUMNS view to list the columns indexed by each index, including those participating in concatenated indexes. The following query lists each table in your schema that contains an index, along with the index name and the column or columns indexed:

```
SELECT table_name,index_name,column_name
FROM user_ind_columns
ORDER BY table_name,index_name,column_position;
```

---

*_INDEXES

Lists all indexes.

OWNER	#VARCHAR2(30)
INDEX_NAME	#VARCHAR2(30)
INDEX_TYPE	VARCHAR2(27)
TABLE_OWNER	#VARCHAR2(30)
TABLE_NAME	#VARCHAR2(30)
TABLE_TYPE	VARCHAR2(11)
UNIQUENESS	VARCHAR2(9)
COMPRESSION	VARCHAR2(8)
PREFIX_LENGTH	NUMBER
TABLESPACE_NAME	VARCHAR2(30)
INI_TRANS	NUMBER
MAX_TRANS	NUMBER
INITIAL_EXTENT	NUMBER
NEXT_EXTENT	NUMBER
MIN_EXTENTS	NUMBER
MAX_EXTENTS	NUMBER
PCT_INCREASE	NUMBER
PCT_THRESHOLD	NUMBER
INCLUDE_COLUMN	NUMBER
FREELISTS	NUMBER

FREELIST_GROUPS	NUMBER
PCT_FREE	NUMBER
LOGGING	VARCHAR2(3)
BLEVEL	NUMBER
LEAF_BLOCKS	NUMBER
DISTINCT_KEYS	NUMBER
AVG_LEAF_BLOCKS_PER_KEY	NUMBER
AVG_DATA_BLOCKS_PER_KEY	NUMBER
CLUSTERING_FACTOR	NUMBER
STATUS	VARCHAR2(8)
NUM_ROWS	NUMBER
SAMPLE_SIZE	NUMBER
LAST_ANALYZED	DATE
DEGREE	VARCHAR2(40)
INSTANCES	VARCHAR2(40)
PARTITIONED	VARCHAR2(3)
TEMPORARY	VARCHAR2(1)
GENERATED	VARCHAR2(1)
SECONDARY	VARCHAR2(1)
BUFFER_POOL	VARCHAR2(7)
USER_STATS	VARCHAR2(3)
DURATION	VARCHAR2(15)
PCT_DIRECT_ACCESS	NUMBER
ITYP_OWNER	VARCHAR2(30)
ITYP_NAME	VARCHAR2(30)
PARAMETERS	VARCHAR2(1000)
GLOBAL_STATS	VARCHAR2(3)
DOMIDX_STATUS	VARCHAR2(12)
DOMIDX_OPSTATUS	VARCHAR2(6)
FUNCIDX_STATUS	VARCHAR2(8)
JOIN_INDEX	VARCHAR2(3)

NOTE

You can use the *_INDEXES view to find particular types of indexes. For example, to find all bitmapped indexes in your schema, use a query like this:

```
SELECT index_name, table_name
FROM user_indexes
WHERE index_type='BITMAP';
```

As with any view containing statistical data, the statistics columns (e.g., NUM_ROWS and LEAF_BLOCKS) are populated only after the index has been analyzed.

INDEX_HISTOGRAM

Contains information about the distribution of index keys within the table. Populated for one index at a time by the ANALYZE INDEX ... VALIDATE STRUCTURE command.

REPEAT_COUNT	NUMBER
KEYS_WITH_REPEAT_COUNT	NUMBER

INDEX_STATS

Contains information about the structure of an index. Populated for one index at a time by the ANALYZE INDEX ... VALIDATE STRUCTURE command.

HEIGHT	NUMBER
BLOCKS	NUMBER
NAME	VARCHAR2(30)
PARTITION_NAME	VARCHAR2(30)
LF_ROWS	NUMBER
LF_BLKS	NUMBER
LF_ROWS_LEN	NUMBER
LF_BLK_LEN	NUMBER
BR_ROWS	NUMBER
BR_BLKS	NUMBER
BR_ROWS_LEN	NUMBER
BR_BLK_LEN	NUMBER
DEL_LF_ROWS	NUMBER
DEL_LF_ROWS_LEN	NUMBER
DISTINCT_KEYS	NUMBER
MOST_REPEATED_KEY	NUMBER
BTREE_SPACE	NUMBER
USED_SPACE	NUMBER
PCT_USED	NUMBER
ROWS_PER_KEY	NUMBER
BLKS_GETS_PER_ACCESS	NUMBER
PRE_ROWS	NUMBER
PRE_ROWS_LEN	NUMBER
OPT_CMPR_COUNT	NUMBER
OPT_CMPR_PCTSAVE	NUMBER

*_JOIN_IND_COLUMNS

Describes the columns used in the join that the bitmapped index is associated with. New with Oracle9i.

INDEX_OWNER	#VARCHAR2(30)
INDEX_NAME	#VARCHAR2(30)
INNER_TABLE_OWNER	#VARCHAR2(30)
INNER_TABLE_NAME	#VARCHAR2(30)
INNER_TABLE_COLUMN	#VARCHAR2(30)
OUTER_TABLE_OWNER	#VARCHAR2(30)

```
            OUTER_TABLE_NAME                 #VARCHAR2(30)
            OUTER_TABLE_COLUMN               #VARCHAR2(30)
```

Jobs and Advanced Queuing

The following views provide information about the job queues managed by the Oracle built-in package, DBMS_JOBS. These job queues are used by the replication facilities and by Oracle Enterprise Manager, but are available for use by any application. Views providing information about the message queues are also included here:

*_ATTRIBUTE_TRANSFORMATIONS

Lists all of the transformation functions for these transformations. There is no ALL_ATTRIBUTE_TRANSFORMATIONS view. New with Oracle9i.

```
    TRANSFORMATION_ID                #NUMBER
    OWNER                            #VARCHAR2(30)
    NAME                             #VARCHAR2(30)
    FROM_TYPE                         VARCHAR2(61)
    TO_TYPE                           VARCHAR2(91)
    ATTRIBUTE                        #NUMBER
    ATTRIBUTE_TRANSFORMATION          VARCHAR2(4000)
```

DBA_TRANSFORMATIONS

Provides information about Advanced Queuing message transformations. New with Oracle9i.

```
    TRANSFORMATION_ID                #NUMBER
    OWNER                            #VARCHAR2(30)
    NAME                             #VARCHAR2(30)
    FROM_TYPE                         VARCHAR2(61)
    TO_TYPE                           VARCHAR2(91)
```

*_JOBS

Lists all jobs defined.

```
    JOB                              #NUMBER
    LOG_USER                         #VARCHAR2(30)
    PRIV_USER                        #VARCHAR2(30)
    SCHEMA_USER                      #VARCHAR2(30)
    LAST_DATE                         DATE
    LAST_SEC                          VARCHAR2(8)
    THIS_DATE                         DATE
    THIS_SEC                          VARCHAR2(8)
    NEXT_DATE                        #DATE
    NEXT_SEC                          VARCHAR2(8)
```

TOTAL_TIME	NUMBER
BROKEN	VARCHAR2(1)
INTERVAL	#VARCHAR2(200)
FAILURES	NUMBER
WHAT	VARCHAR2(4000)
NLS_ENV	VARCHAR2(4000)
MISC_ENV	RAW(32)
INSTANCE	NUMBER

*_JOBS_RUNNING

Lists all currently running jobs.

SID	NUMBER
JOB	NUMBER
FAILURES	NUMBER
LAST_DATE	DATE
LAST_SEC	VARCHAR2(8)
THIS_DATE	DATE
THIS_SEC	VARCHAR2(8)
INSTANCE	NUMBER

*_QUEUE_SCHEDULES

Shows when particular queued messages are to be delivered.

SCHEMA	#VARCHAR2(30)
QNAME	#VARCHAR2(30)
DESTINATION	#VARCHAR2(128)
START_DATE	DATE
START_TIME	VARCHAR2(8)
PROPAGATION_WINDOW	NUMBER
NEXT_TIME	VARCHAR2(200)
LATENCY	NUMBER
SCHEDULE_DISABLED	VARCHAR2(1)
PROCESS_NAME	VARCHAR2(8)
SESSION_ID	VARCHAR2(82)
INSTANCE	NUMBER
LAST_RUN_DATE	DATE
LAST_RUN_TIME	VARCHAR2(8)
CURRENT_START_DATE	DATE
CURRENT_START_TIME	VARCHAR2(8)
NEXT_RUN_DATE	DATE
NEXT_RUN_TIME	VARCHAR2(8)
TOTAL_TIME	NUMBER
TOTAL_NUMBER	NUMBER
TOTAL_BYTES	NUMBER
MAX_NUMBER	NUMBER
MAX_BYTES	NUMBER
AVG_NUMBER	NUMBER
AVG_SIZE	NUMBER
AVG_TIME	NUMBER

FAILURES	NUMBER
LAST_ERROR_DATE	DATE
LAST_ERROR_TIME	VARCHAR2(8)
LAST_ERROR_MSG	VARCHAR2(4000)

*_QUEUE_TABLES

Lists the tables used to hold the queues defined as part of the Oracle Advanced Queuing facility.

OWNER	VARCHAR2(30)
QUEUE_TABLE	VARCHAR2(30)
TYPE	VARCHAR2(7)
OBJECT_TYPE	VARCHAR2(61)
SORT_ORDER	VARCHAR2(22)
RECIPIENTS	VARCHAR2(8)
MESSAGE_GROUPING	VARCHAR2(13)
COMPATIBLE	VARCHAR2(5)
PRIMARY_INSTANCE	NUMBER
SECONDARY_INSTANCE	NUMBER
OWNER_INSTANCE	NUMBER
USER_COMMENT	VARCHAR2(50)
SECURE	VARCHAR2(3)

*_QUEUES

Lists the queues defined as part of the Advanced Queuing facility.

OWNER	#VARCHAR2(30)
NAME	#VARCHAR2(30)
QUEUE_TABLE	#VARCHAR2(30)
QID	#NUMBER
QUEUE_TYPE	VARCHAR2(20)
MAX_RETRIES	NUMBER
RETRY_DELAY	NUMBER
ENQUEUE_ENABLED	VARCHAR2(7)
DEQUEUE_ENABLED	VARCHAR2(7)
RETENTION	VAKLHAR2(40)
USER_COMMENT	VARCHAR2(50)

Locks

The following views provide information about the current status of locks in the database:

*_BLOCKERS

Lists all sessions holding locks for whose release others are waiting.

HOLDING_SESSION	NUMBER

DBMS_LOCK_ALLOCATED

Shows which locks the current user has allocated.

NAME	#VARCHAR2(128)
LOCKID	NUMBER(38)
EXPIRATION	DATE

*_DDL_LOCKS

Lists all existing DDL locks.

SESSION_ID	NUMBER
OWNER	VARCHAR2(30)
NAME	VARCHAR2(30)
TYPE	VARCHAR2(40)
MODE_HELD	VARCHAR2(9)
MODE_REQUESTED	VARCHAR2(9)

*_DML_LOCKS

Lists all existing DML locks.

SESSION_ID	NUMBER
OWNER	#VARCHAR2(30)
NAME	#VARCHAR2(30)
MODE_HELD	VARCHAR2(13)
MODE_REQUESTED	VARCHAR2(13)
LAST_CONVERT	NUMBER
BLOCKING_OTHERS	VARCHAR2(40)

*_KGLLOCK

Lists all Kernel Generic Library (KGL) cache locks in the database.

KGLLKUSE	RAW(4)
KGLLKHDL	RAW(4)
KGLLKMOD	NUMBER
KGLLKREQ	NUMBER
KGLLKTYPE	VARCHAR2(4)

*_LOCK

Lists all locks held or requested in the database.

SESSION_ID	NUMBER
LOCK_TYPE	VARCHAR2(26)
MODE_HELD	VARCHAR2(40)

MODE_REQUESTED	VARCHAR2(40)
LOCK_ID1	VARCHAR2(40)
LOCK_ID2	VARCHAR2(40)
LAST_CONVERT	NUMBER
BLOCKING_OTHERS	VARCHAR2(40)

*_LOCK_INTERNAL

Contains internal information for locks defined in *_LOCKS.

SESSION_ID	NUMBER
LOCK_TYPE	VARCHAR2(56)
MODE_HELD	VARCHAR2(40)
MODE_REQUESTED	VARCHAR2(40)
LOCK_ID1	VARCHAR2(1130)
LOCK_ID2	VARCHAR2(40)

*_WAITERS

Lists all sessions that are waiting on a lock held by another session.

WAITING_SESSION	NUMBER
HOLDING_SESSION	NUMBER
LOCK_TYPE	VARCHAR2(26)
MODE_HELD	VARCHAR2(40)
MODE_REQUESTED	VARCHAR2(40)
LOCK_ID1	NUMBER
LOCK_ID2	NUMBER

Log groups

A log group is used to multiplex log files across different locations. It contains multiple members, which are identical log files. You can use log groups to reduce the impact of a disk failure disaster on the recovery process:

*_LOG_GROUP_COLUMNS

Lists the columns assigned to log groups. New with Oracle9i.

OWNER	#VARCHAR2(30)
LOG_GROUP_NAME	#VARCHAR2(30)
TABLE_NAME	#VARCHAR2(30)
COLUMN_NAME	VARCHAR2(4000)
POSITION	NUMBER

*_LOG_GROUPS

Lists the tables that are associated with log groups. New with Oracle9i.

OWNER	#VARCHAR2(30)
LOG_GROUP_NAME	#VARCHAR2(30)
TABLE_NAME	#VARCHAR2(30)
ALWAYS	VARCHAR2(6)

Materialized views

A materialized view speeds up data warehouse queries with precalculated aggregates. The following views provide information about materialized views:

*_BASE_TABLE_MVIEWS

Lists information about existing materialized views.

OWNER	VARCHAR2(30)
MASTER	VARCHAR2(30)
MVIEW_LAST_REFRESH_TIME	DATE
MVIEW_ID	NUMBER

*_MVIEW_LOGS

Lists information about materialized view logs that track changes to the master tables, which can be used to refresh the materialized views.

LOG_OWNER	VARCHAR2(30)
MASTER	VARCHAR2(30)
LOG_TABLE	VARCHAR2(30)
LOG_TRIGGER	VARCHAR2(30)
ROWIDS	VARCHAR2(3)
PRIMARY_KEY	VARCHAR2(3)
OBJECT_ID	VARCHAR2(3)
FILTER_COLUMNS	VARCHAR2(3)
SEQUENCE	VARCHAR2(3)
INCLUDE_NEW_VALUES	VARCHAR2(3)

Networking and distributed transactions

The following views provide information about the status of Oracle networking, remote databases, and distributed transactions to these remote databases:

*_2PC_NEIGHBORS

Contains information about the commit point for distributed transactions listed in *_2PC_PENDING.

LOCAL_TRAN_ID	VARCHAR2(22)
IN_OUT	VARCHAR2(3)
DATABASE	VARCHAR2(128)
DBUSER_OWNER	VARCHAR2(30)
INTERFACE	VARCHAR2(1)
DBID	VARCHAR2(16)
SESS#	NUMBER(38)
BRANCH	VARCHAR2(128)

*_2PC_PENDING

Lists information about distributed transactions requiring recovery.

LOCAL_TRAN_ID	#VARCHAR2(22)
GLOBAL_TRAN_ID	VARCHAR2(169)
STATE	#VARCHAR2(16)
MIXED	VARCHAR2(3)
ADVICE	VARCHAR2(1)
TRAN_COMMENT	VARCHAR2(255)
FAIL_TIME #DATE	
FORCE_TIME DATE	
RETRY_TIME	#DATE
OS_USER	VARCHAR2(64)
OS_TERMINAL	VARCHAR2(255)
HOST	VARCHAR2(128)
DB_USER	VARCHAR2(30)
COMMIT#	VARCHAR2(16)

*_DB_LINKS

Lists all database links.

OWNER	#VARCHAR2(30)
DB_LINK	#VARCHAR2(128)
USERNAME	VARCHAR2(30)
HOST	VARCHAR2(2000)
CREATED	#DATE

NOTE

Notice that this is a secure way to view the database links, because the password column (which is part of the underlying SYS view) is not displayed.

GLOBAL_NAME

Shows the value of the global name. Can be used to determine which database the application is connected to.

GLOBAL_NAME	VARCHAR2(4000)

NOTE

While it might appear that the GLOBAL_NAME view is related to the initialization parameter GLOBAL_NAMES, that is not the case. GLOBAL_NAMES will contain a valid value even if the initialization parameter GLOBAL_NAMES is set to FALSE.

---

*_PENDING_TRANSACTIONS

Contains further information used by XA for distributed transactions listed in *_2PC_PENDING.

FORMATID	NUMBER
GLOBALID	RAW(64)
BRANCHID	RAW(64)

TRUSTED_SERVERS

Specifies which servers have been identified as trusted.

TRUST	VARCHAR2(9)
NAME	VARCHAR2(128)

Objects Option

The following views provide information relating to objects created using Oracle's Objects Option, including Large Objects (LOBs):

*_COLL_TYPES

Lists collection types created.

OWNER	#VARCHAR2(30)
TYPE_NAME	#VARCHAR2(30)
COLL_TYPE	#VARCHAR2(30)
UPPER_BOUND	NUMBER
ELEM_TYPE_MOD	VARCHAR2(7)
ELEM_TYPE_OWNER	VARCHAR2(30)
ELEM_TYPE_NAME	VARCHAR2(30)
LENGTH	NUMBER
PRECISION	NUMBER
SCALE	NUMBER
CHARACTER_SET_NAME	VARCHAR2(44)
ELEM_STORAGE	VARCHAR2(7)
NULLS_STORED	VARCHAR2(3)

*_DIRECTORIES

Lists all defined external directories where BFILEs are stored.

OWNER	#VARCHAR2(30)
DIRECTORY_NAME	#VARCHAR2(30)
DIRECTORY_PATH	VARCHAR2(4000)

*_LOBS

Lists all large objects defined in the database.

OWNER	VARCHAR2(30)
TABLE_NAME	VARCHAR2(30)
COLUMN_NAME	VARCHAR2(4000)
SEGMENT_NAME	VARCHAR2(30)
INDEX_NAME	VARCHAR2(30)
CHUNK	NUMBER
PCTVERSION	NUMBER
RETENTION	NUMBER
FREEPOOLS	NUMBER
CACHE	VARCHAR2(10)
LOGGING	VARCHAR2(7)
IN_ROW	VARCHAR2(3)

*_METHOD_PARAMS

Lists all parameters for methods defined in *_TYPE_ METHODS.

OWNER	#VARCHAR2(30)
TYPE_NAME	#VARCHAR2(30)
METHOD_NAME	#VARCHAR2(30)
METHOD_NO	#NUMBER
PARAM_NAME	#VARCHAR2(30)
PARAM_NO	#NUMBER
PARAM_MODE	VARCHAR2(6)
PARAM_TYPE_MOD	VARCHAR2(7)
PARAM_TYPE_OWNER	VARCHAR2(30)
PARAM_TYPE_NAME	VARCHAR2(30)
CHARACTER_SET_NAME	VARCHAR2(44)

*_METHOD_RESULTS

Lists all method results for methods defined in *_TYPE_ METHODS.

OWNER	#VARCHAR2(30)
TYPE_NAME	#VARCHAR2(30)
METHOD_NAME	#VARCHAR2(30)
METHOD_NO	#NUMBER
RESULT_TYPE_MOD	VARCHAR2(7)
RESULT_TYPE_OWNER	VARCHAR2(30)
RESULT_TYPE_NAME	VARCHAR2(30)
CHARACTER_SET_NAME	VARCHAR2(44)

*_NESTED_TABLES

Lists all nested tables created using features from the Objects Option.

OWNER	VARCHAR2(30)
TABLE_NAME	VARCHAR2(30)
TABLE_TYPE_OWNER	VARCHAR2(30)
TABLE_TYPE_NAME	VARCHAR2(30)
PARENT_TABLE_NAME	VARCHAR2(30)
PARENT_TABLE_COLUMN	VARCHAR2(4000)
STORAGE_SPEC	VARCHAR2(30)
RETURN_TYPE	VARCHAR2(20)
ELEMENT_SUBSTITUTABLE	VARCHAR2(25)

*_OBJECT_TABLES

Lists all tables created using features from the Objects Option.

OWNER	#VARCHAR2(30)
TABLE_NAME	#VARCHAR2(30)
TABLESPACE_NAME	VARCHAR2(30)

CLUSTER_NAME	VARCHAR2(30)
IOT_NAME	VARCHAR2(30)
PCT_FREE	NUMBER
PCT_USED	NUMBER
INI_TRANS	NUMBER
MAX_TRANS	NUMBER
INITIAL_EXTENT	NUMBER
NEXT_EXTENT	NUMBER
MIN_EXTENTS	NUMBER
MAX_EXTENTS	NUMBER
PCT_INCREASE	NUMBER
FREELISTS	NUMBER
FREELIST_GROUPS	NUMBER
LOGGING	VARCHAR2(3)
BACKED_UP	VARCHAR2(1)
NUM_ROWS	NUMBER
BLOCKS	NUMBER
EMPTY_BLOCKS	NUMBER
AVG_SPACE	NUMBER
CHAIN_CNT	NUMBER
AVG_ROW_LEN	NUMBER
AVG_SPACE_FREELIST_BLOCKS	NUMBER
NUM_FREELIST_BLOCKS	NUMBER
DEGREE	VARCHAR2(10)
INSTANCES	VARCHAR2(10)
CACHE	VARCHAR2(5)
TABLE_LOCK	VARCHAR2(8)
SAMPLE_SIZE	NUMBER
LAST_ANALYZED	DATE
PARTITIONED	VARCHAR2(3)
IOT_TYPE	VARCHAR2(12)
OBJECT_ID_TYPE	VARCHAR2(16)
TABLE_TYPE_OWNER	VARCHAR2(30)
TABLE_TYPE	VARCHAR2(30)
TEMPORARY	VARCHAR2(1)
SECONDARY	VARCHAR2(1)
NESTED	VARCHAR2(3)
BUFFER_POOL	VARCHAR2(7)
ROW_MOVEMENT	VARCHAR2(8)
GLOBAL_STATS	VARCHAR2(3)
USER_STATS	VARCHAR2(3)
DURATION	VARCHAR2(15)
SKIP_CORRUPT	VARCHAR2(8)
MONITORING	VARCHAR2(3)
CLUSTER_OWNER	VARCHAR2(30)
DEPENDENCIES	VARCHAR2(8)

*_REFS

Lists the REF columns and attributes for objects.

OWNER	#VARCHAR2(30)
TABLE_NAME	#VARCHAR2(30)
COLUMN_NAME	VARCHAR2(4000)
WITH_ROWID	VARCHAR2(3)
IS_SCOPED	VARCHAR2(3)
SCOPE_TABLE_OWNER	VARCHAR2(30)
SCOPE_TABLE_NAME	VARCHAR2(30)
OBJECT_ID_TYPE	VARCHAR2(33)

*_TYPE_ATTRS

Lists attributes of all types.

OWNER	VARCHAR2(30)
TYPE_NAME	#VARCHAR2(30)
ATTR_NAME	#VARCHAR2(30)
ATTR_TYPE_MOD	VARCHAR2(7)
ATTR_TYPE_OWNER	VARCHAR2(30)
ATTR_TYPE_NAME	VARCHAR2(30)
LENGTH	NUMBER
PRECISION	NUMBER
SCALE	NUMBER
CHARACTER_SET_NAME	VARCHAR2(44)
ATTR_NO	#NUMBER
INHERITED	VARCHAR2(3)

*_TYPE_METHODS

Lists methods created to support types defined in *_TYPES.

OWNER	#VARCHAR2(30)
TYPE_NAME	#VARCHAR2(30)
METHOD_NAME	#VARCHAR2(30)
METHOD_NO	#NUMBER
METHOD_TYPE	VARCHAR2(6)
PARAMETERS	#NUMBER
RESULTS	#NUMBER
FINAL	VARCHAR2(3)
INSTANTIABLE	VARCHAR2(3)
OVERRIDING	VARCHAR2(3)
INHERITED	VARCHAR2(3)

*_TYPES

Lists all types created.

OWNER	VARCHAR2(30)
TYPE_NAME	#VARCHAR2(30)
TYPE_OID	#RAW(16)
TYPECODE	VARCHAR2(30)
ATTRIBUTES	NUMBER

METHODS	NUMBER
PREDEFINED	VARCHAR2(3)
INCOMPLETE	VARCHAR2(3)
FINAL	VARCHAR2(3)
INSTANTIABLE	VARCHAR2(3)
SUPERTYPE_OWNER	VARCHAR2(30)
SUPERTYPE_NAME	VARCHAR2(30)
LOCAL_ATTRIBUTES	NUMBER
LOCAL_METHODS	NUMBER
TYPEID	RAW(16)

Partitioning

The following views provide information about partitioned tables and indexes.

*_IND_PARTITIONS

Lists all index partitions. There's one row for each index partition.

INDEX_OWNER	VARCHAR2(30)
INDEX_NAME	VARCHAR2(30)
COMPOSITE	VARCHAR2(3)
PARTITION_NAME	VARCHAR2(30)
SUBPARTITION_COUNT	NUMBER
HIGH_VALUE	LONG
HIGH_VALUE_LENGTH	NUMBER
PARTITION_POSITION	NUMBER
STATUS	VARCHAR2(8)
TABLESPACE_NAME	VARCHAR2(30)
PCT_FREE	NUMBER
INI_TRANS	NUMBER
MAX_TRANS	NUMBER
INITIAL_EXTENT	NUMBER
NEXT_EXTENT	NUMBER
MIN_EXTENT	NUMBER
MAX_EXTENT	NUMBER
PCT_INCREASE	NUMBER
FREELISTS	NUMBER
FREELIST_GROUPS	NUMBER
LOGGING	VARCHAR2(7)
COMPRESSION	VARCHAR2(8)
BLEVEL	NUMBER
LEAF_BLOCKS	NUMBER
DISTINCT_KEYS	NUMBER
AVG_LEAF_BLOCKS_PER_KEY	NUMBER
AVG_DATA_BLOCKS_PER_KEY	NUMBER
CLUSTERING_FACTOR	NUMBER
NUM_ROWS	NUMBER
SAMPLE_SIZE	NUMBER

LAST_ANALYZED	DATE
BUFFER_POOL	VARCHAR2(7)
USER_STATS	VARCHAR2(3)
PCT_DIRECT_ACCESS	NUMBER
GLOBAL_STATS	VARCHAR2(3)
DOMIDX_OPSTATUS	VARCHAR2(6)
PARAMETERS	VARCHAR2(1000)

*_IND_SUBPARTITIONS

Lists all index subpartitions. There is one row for each index subpartition.

INDEX_OWNER	#VARCHAR2(30)
INDEX_NAME	#VARCHAR2(30)
PARTITION_NAME	VARCHAR2(30)
SUBPARTITION_NAME	VARCHAR2(30)
HIGH_VALUE	LONG
HIGH_VALUE_LENGTH	#NUMBER
SUBPARTITION_POSITION	#NUMBER
STATUS	VARCHAR2(8)
TABLESPACE_NAME	#VARCHAR2(30)
PCT_FREE	#NUMBER
INI_TRANS	#NUMBER
MAX_TRANS	#NUMBER
INITIAL_EXTENT	NUMBER
NEXT_EXTENT	NUMBER
MIN_EXTENT	#NUMBER
MAX_EXTENT	#NUMBER
PCT_INCREASE	NUMBER
FREELISTS	NUMBER
FREELIST_GROUPS	NUMBER
LOGGING	VARCHAR2(3)
BLEVEL	NUMBER
LEAF_BLOCKS	NUMBER
DISTINCT_KEYS	NUMBER
AVG_LEAF_BLOCKS_PER_KEY	NUMBER
AVG_DATA_BLOCKS_PER_KEY	NUMBER
CLUSTERING_FACTOR	NUMBER
NUM_ROWS	NUMBER
SAMPLE_SIZE	NUMBER
LAST_ANALYZED	DATE
BUFFER_POOL	VARCHAR2(7)
USER_STATS	VARCHAR2(3)
GLOBAL_STATS	VARCHAR2(3)

*_PART_COL_STATISTICS

Contains distribution information about partitioned columns that have been analyzed—for example, *_TAB_COL_STATISTICS for partitioned tables.

OWNER	#VARCHAR2(30)
TABLE_NAME	#VARCHAR2(30)
PARTITION_NAME	VARCHAR2(30)
COLUMN_NAME	VARCHAR2(4000)
NUM_DISTINCT	NUMBER
LOW_VALUE	RAW(32)
HIGH_VALUE	RAW(32)
DENSITY	NUMBER
NUM_NULLS	NUMBER
NUM_BUCKETS	NUMBER
SAMPLE_SIZE	NUMBER
LAST_ANALYZED	DATE
GLOBAL_STATS	VARCHAR2(3)
USER_STATS	VARCHAR2(3)
AVG_COL_LEN	NUMBER

*_PART_HISTOGRAMS

Contains information about histograms created on individual partitions.

OWNER	VARCHAR2(30)
TABLE_NAME	VARCHAR2(30)
PARTITION_NAME	VARCHAR2(30)
COLUMN_NAME	VARCHAR2(4000)
BUCKET_NUMBER	NUMBER
ENDPOINT_VALUE	NUMBER
ENDPOINT_ACTUAL_VALUE	VARCHAR2(1000)

*_PART_INDEXES

Lists all partitioned indexes. There is one row for each partitioned index.

OWNER	#VARCHAR2(30)
INDEX_NAME	#VARCHAR2(30)
TABLE_NAME	#VARCHAR2(30)
PARTITIONING_TYPE	VARCHAR2(7)
SUBPARTITIONING_TYPE	VARCHAR2(7)
PARTITION_COUNT	#NUMBER
DEF_SUBPARTITION_COUNT	NUMBER
PARTITIONING_KEY_COUNT	#NUMBER
SUBPARTITIONING_KEY_COUNT	NUMBER
LOCALITY	VARCHAR2(6)
ALIGNMENT	VARCHAR2(12)
DEF_TABLESPACE_NAME	VARCHAR2(30)
DEF_PCT_FREE	#NUMBER
DEF_INI_TRANS	#NUMBER
DEF_MAX_TRANS	#NUMBER
DEF_INITIAL_EXTENT	VARCHAR2(40)
DEF_NEXT_EXTENT	VARCHAR2(40)
DEF_MIN_EXTENTS	VARCHAR2(40)

DEF_MAX_EXTENTS	VARCHAR2(40)
DEF_PCT_INCREASE	VARCHAR2(40)
DEF_FREELISTS	#NUMBER
DEF_FREELIST_GROUPS	#NUMBER
DEF_LOGGING	VARCHAR2(7)
DEF_BUFFER_POOL	VARCHAR2(7)
DEF_PARAMETERS	VARCHAR2(1000)

*_PART_KEY_COLUMNS

Lists the partition key columns for all partitions.

OWNER	VARCHAR2(30)
NAME	VARCHAR2(30)
OBJECT_TYPE	CHAR(5)
COLUMN_NAME	VARCHAR2(4000)
COLUMN_POSITION	NUMBER

*_PART_TABLES

Lists all partitioned tables. There is one row for each partitioned table.

OWNER	VARCHAR2(30)
TABLE_NAME	VARCHAR2(30)
PARTITIONING_TYPE	VARCHAR2(7)
SUBPARTITIONING_TYPE	VARCHAR2(7)
PARTITION_COUNT	NUMBER
DEF_SUBPARTITION_COUNT	NUMBER
PARTITIONING_KEY_COUNT	NUMBER
SUBPARTITIONING_KEY_COUNT	NUMBER
DEF_TABLESPACE_NAME	VARCHAR2(30)
DEF_PCT_FREE	NUMBER
DEF_PCT_USED	NUMBER
DEF_INI_TRANS	NUMBER
DEF_MAX_TRANS	NUMBER
DEF_INITIAL_EXTENT	VARCHAR2(40)
DEF_NEXT_EXTENT	VARCHAR2(40)
DEF_MIN_EXTENTS	VARCHAR2(40)
DEF_MAX_EXTENTS	VARCHAR2(40)
DEF_PCT_INCREASE	VARCHAR2(40)
DEF_FREELISTS	NUMBER
DEF_FREELIST_GROUPS	NUMBER
DEF_LOGGING	VARCHAR2(7)
DEF_COMPRESSION	VARCHAR2(8)
DEF_BUFFER_POOL	VARCHAR2(7)

*_TAB_PARTITIONS

Lists all table partitions. There is one row for each table partition.

TABLE_OWNER	VARCHAR2(30)
TABLE_NAME	VARCHAR2(30)
COMPOSITE	VARCHAR2(3)
PARTITION_NAME	VARCHAR2(30)
SUBPARTITION_COUNT	NUMBER
HIGH_VALUE	LONG
HIGH_VALUE_LENGTH	NUMBER
PARTITION_POSITION	NUMBER
TABLESPACE_NAME	VARCHAR2(30)
PCT_FREE	NUMBER
PCT_USED	NUMBER
INI_TRANS	NUMBER
MAX_TRANS	NUMBER
INITIAL_EXTENT	NUMBER
NEXT_EXTENT	NUMBER
MIN_EXTENT	NUMBER
MAX_EXTENT	NUMBER
PCT_INCREASE	NUMBER
FREELISTS	NUMBER
FREELIST_GROUPS	NUMBER
LOGGING	VARCHAR2(7)
COMPRESSION	VARCHAR2(8)
NUM_ROWS	NUMBER
BLOCKS	NUMBER
EMPTY_BLOCKS	NUMBER
AVG_SPACE	NUMBER
CHAIN_CNT	NUMBER
AVG_ROW_LEN	NUMBER
SAMPLE_SIZE	NUMBER
LAST_ANALYZED	DATE
BUFFER_POOL	VARCHAR2(7)
GLOBAL_STATS	VARCHAR2(3)
USER_STATS	VARCHAR2(3)

*_TAB_SUBPARTITIONS

Lists all table subpartitions. There is one row for each table subpartition.

TABLE_OWNER	#VARCHAR2(30)
TABLE_NAME	#VARCHAR2(30)
PARTITION_NAME	VARCHAR2(30)
SUBPARTITION_NAME	VARCHAR2(30)
HIGH_VALUE	LONG
HIGH_VALUE_LENGTH	#NUMBER
SUBPARTITION_POSITION	#NUMBER
TABLESPACE_NAME	#VARCHAR2(30)
PCT_FREE	#NUMBER
PCT_USED	NUMBER
INI_TRANS	#NUMBER
MAX_TRANS	#NUMBER

INITIAL_EXTENT	NUMBER
NEXT_EXTENT	NUMBER
MIN_EXTENT	#NUMBER
MAX_EXTENT	#NUMBER
PCT_INCREASE	NUMBER
FREELISTS	NUMBER
FREELIST_GROUPS	NUMBER
LOGGING	VARCHAR2(3)
COMPRESSION	VARCHAR2(8)
NUM_ROWS	NUMBER
BLOCKS	NUMBER
EMPTY_BLOCKS	NUMBER
AVG_SPACE	NUMBER
CHAIN_CNT	NUMBER
AVG_ROW_LEN	NUMBER
SAMPLE_SIZE	NUMBER
LAST_ANALYZED	DATE
BUFFER_POOL	VARCHAR2(7)
GLOBAL_STATS	VARCHAR2(3)
USER_STATS	VARCHAR2(3)

Programming and PL/SQL

The following views provide information about PL/SQL stored programs, including functions, procedures, packages, and triggers:

*_ARGUMENTS

Lists all valid arguments for stored procedures and functions. There is no DBA_ARGUMENTS view.

OWNER	#VARCHAR2(30)
OBJECT_NAME	VARCHAR2(30)
PACKAGE_NAME	VARCHAR2(30)
OBJECT_ID	#NUMBER
OVERLOAD	VARCHAR2(40)
ARGUMENT_NAME	VARCHAR2(30)
POSITION	#NUMBER
SEQUENCE	#NUMBER
DATA_LEVEL	#NUMBER
DATA_TYPE	VARCHAR2(30)
DEFAULT_VALUE	LONG
DEFAULT_LENGTH	NUMBER
IN_OUT	VARCHAR2(9)
DATA_LENGTH	NUMBER
DATA_PRECISION	NUMBER
DATA_SCALE	NUMBER
RADIX	NUMBER

CHARACTER_SET_NAME	VARCHAR2(44)
TYPE_OWNER	VARCHAR2(30)
TYPE_NAME	VARCHAR2(30)
TYPE_SUBNAME	VARCHAR2(30)
TYPE_LINK	VARCHAR2(128)
PLS_TYPE	VARCHAR2(30)
CHAR_LENGTH	NUMBER
CHAR_USED	VARCHAR2(1)

NOTE

You may wish to use the *_ARGUMENTS view as a tool to help standardize argument names. By issuing a query such as:

```
SELECT argument_name,data_type,data_length,object_name
FROM user_arguments
ORDER BY argument_name
```

You easily see arguments with the same name and the object with which they are used. By also examining the data type and length, you'll know if arguments with the same name are likely to actually represent the same argument.

---

*_ERRORS

Shows all errors from compiling objects.

OWNER	#VARCHAR2(30)
NAME	#VARCHAR2(30)
TYPE	VARCHAR2(12)
SEQUENCE	#NUMBER
LINE	#NUMBER
POSITION	#NUMBER
TEXT	#VARCHAR2(4000)

NOTE

While the SQL*Plus SHOW ERRORS command will display errors on a just-compiled PL/SQL procedure, the *_ERRORS view is much more robust and provides detailed information on all current errors.

---

*_LIBRARIES

Lists the external libraries that can be called from PL/SQL packages, procedures, and functions.

OWNER	#VARCHAR2(30)
LIBRARY_NAME	#VARCHAR2(30)
FILE_SPEC	VARCHAR2(2000)
DYNAMIC	VARCHAR2(1)
STATUS	VARCHAR2(7)

*_OBJECT_SIZE

Shows the size of the compiled code for each PL/SQL package, procedure, function, and trigger.

OWNER	#VARCHAR2(30)
NAME	#VARCHAR2(30)
TYPE	VARCHAR2(13)
SOURCE_SIZE	NUMBER
PARSED_SIZE	NUMBER
CODE_SIZE	NUMBER
ERROR_SIZE	NUMBER

*_PROCEDURES

Lists information about procedures defined within the database, such as whether they are aggregate functions, pipelined table functions, or parallel-enabled functions. New with Oracle9i.

OWNER	#VARCHAR2(30)
OBJECT_NAME	#VARCHAR2(30)
PROCEDURE_NAME	VARCHAR2(30)
AGGREGATE	VARCHAR2(3)
PIPELINED	VARCHAR2(3)
IMPLTYPEOWNER	VARCHAR2(30)
IMPLTYPENAME	VARCHAR2(30)
PARALLEL	VARCHAR2(3)
INTERFACE	VARCHAR2(3)
DETERMINISTIC	VARCHAR2(3)
AUTHID	VARCHAR2(12)

PUBLIC_DEPENDENCY

Lists dependencies using only object numbers.

| OBJECT_ID | #NUMBER |
| REFERENCED_OBJECT_ID | #NUMBER |

*_SOURCE

Shows PL/SQL source for packages, procedures, and functions.

OWNER	VARCHAR2(30)
NAME	VARCHAR2(30)
TYPE	VARCHAR2(12)
LINE	NUMBER
TEXT	VARCHAR2(4000)

Use the *_SOURCE view to list the source code for any type
of stored object in the database. To list the source for a particular trigger in your schema, use a query like this one:

```
SELECT text
FROM user_source
WHERE name='trigger_name'
AND type='TRIGGER'
ORDER BY line
```

Note that the final line is used to sequence the output,
and the text is stored as a LONG, so you'll need to allocate sufficient buffer space (e.g., specify SET LONG 4000
in SQL*Plus).

*_STORED_SETTINGS

Provides information about persistent parameter settings for
stored PL/SQL units. New with Oracle9i.

OWNER	#VARCHAR2(30)
OBJECT_NAME	#VARCHAR2(30)
OBJECT_ID	#NUMBER
OBJECT_TYPE	VARCHAR2(12)
PARAM_NAME	#VARCHAR2(30)
PARAM_VALUE	VARCHAR2(4000)

*_TRIGGER_COLS

Lists columns that are referenced in triggers.

TRIGGER_OWNER	VARCHAR2(30)
TRIGGER_NAME	VARCHAR2(30)
TABLE_OWNER	VARCHAR2(30)
TABLE_NAME	VARCHAR2(30)
COLUMN_NAME	VARCHAR2(4000)
COLUMN_LIST	VARCHAR2(3)
COLUMN_USAGE	VARCHAR2(17)

*_TRIGGERS

Shows PL/SQL code for database triggers.

OWNER	VARCHAR2(30)
TRIGGER_NAME	VARCHAR2(30)
TRIGGER_TYPE	VARCHAR2(16)
TRIGGERING_EVENT	VARCHAR2(227)
TABLE_OWNER	VARCHAR2(30)
BASE_OBJECT_TYPE	VARCHAR2(16)
TABLE_NAME	VARCHAR2(30)

COLUMN_NAME	VARCHAR2(4000)
REFERENCING_NAMES	VARCHAR2(128)
WHEN_CLAUSE	VARCHAR2(4000)
STATUS	VARCHAR2(8)
DESCRIPTION	VARCHAR2(4000)
ACTION_TYPE	VARCHAR2(11)
TRIGGER_BODY	LONG

Replication

The following views provide information used by Oracle's advanced replication facilities. Oracle currently recommends using the Replication Manager to obtain the information in these views:

DBA_REPEXTENSIONS

Lists current operations that are adding new master sites to a master group without quiescing the master group. New with Oracle9*i*.

EXTENSION_ID	#RAW(16)
REQUEST	VARCHAR2(15)
MASTERDEF	VARCHAR2(128)
EXPORT_REQUIRED	VARCHAR2(3)
REPCATLOG_ID	NUMBER
EXTENSION_STATUS	VARCHAR2(13)
FLASHBACK_SCN	NUMBER
BREAK_TRANS_TO_MASTERDEF	VARCHAR2(3)
BREAK_TRANS_TO_NEW_MASTERS	VARCHAR2(3)
PERCENTAGE_FOR_CATCHUP_MDEF	NUMBER
CYCLE_SECONDS_MDEF	NUMBER
PERCENTAGE_FOR_CATCHUP_NEW	NUMBER
CYCLE_SECONDS_NEW	NUMBER

DBA_REPSITES_NEW

Lists the new replication sites that you plan to add to your replication environment. New with Oracle9*i*.

EXTENSION_ID	#RAW(16)
GOWNER	#VARCHAR2(30)
GNAME	#VARCHAR2(30)
DBLINK	#VARCHAR2(128)
FULL_INSTANTIATION	VARCHAR2(1)
MASTER_STATUS	VARCHAR2(13)

DEFCALLDEST

Lists destinations for each deferred remote procedure call. New with Oracle9*i*.

```
CALLNO                      #NUMBER
DEFERRED_TRAN_ID            #VARCHAR2(30)
DBLINK                      #VARCHAR2(128)
```

*_REGISTERED_MVIEW_GROUPS

Lists registered materialized view groups.

```
NAME                        VARCHAR2(30)
MVIEW_SITE                  VARCHAR2(128)
GROUP_COMMENT               VARCHAR2(80)
VERSION                     VARCHAR2(8)
FNAME                       VARCHAR2(30)
OWNER                       VARCHAR2(30)
```

*_REGISTERED_MVIEWS

Lists registered materialized views.

```
OWNER                       #VARCHAR2(30)
NAME                        #VARCHAR2(30)
MVIEW_SITE                  #VARCHAR2(128)
CAN_USE_LOG                 VARCHAR2(3)
UPDATABLE                   VARCHAR2(3)
REFRESH_METHOD              VARCHAR2(11)
MVIEW_ID                    NUMBER(38)
VERSION                     VARCHAR2(26)
QUERY_TXT                   LONG
```

*_REGISTERED_SNAPSHOT_GROUPS

Lists registered snapshot groups.

```
NAME                        VARCHAR2(30)
SNAPSHOT_SITE               VARCHAR2(128)
GROUP_COMMENT               VARCHAR2(80)
VERSION                     VARCHAR2(8)
FNAME                       VARCHAR2(30)
OWNER                       VARCHAR2(30)
```

*_REGISTERED_SNAPSHOTS

Lists registered snapshots.

```
OWNER                       #VARCHAR2(30)
NAME                        #VARCHAR2(30)
SNAPSHOT_SITE               #VARCHAR2(128)
CAN_USE_LOG                 VARCHAR2(3)
UPDATABLE                   VARCHAR2(3)
REFRESH_METHOD              VARCHAR2(11)
SNAPSHOT_ID                 NUMBER(38)
VERSION                     VARCHAR2(17)
QUERY_TXT                   LONG
```

*_REPAUDIT_ATTRIBUTE

Lists replication audit attributes.

ATTRIBUTE	#VARCHAR2(30)
DATA_TYPE	VARCHAR2(9)
DATA_LENGTH	NUMBER(38)
SOURCE	#VARCHAR2(92)

*_REPAUDIT_COLUMN

Lists replication audit columns.

SNAME	#VARCHAR2(30)
ONAME	#VARCHAR2(30)
COLUMN_NAME	#VARCHAR2(30)
BASE_SNAME	#VARCHAR2(30)
BASE_ONAME	#VARCHAR2(30)
BASE_CONFLICT_TYPE	VARCHAR2(10)
BASE_REFERENCE_NAME	#VARCHAR2(30)
ATTRIBUTE	#VARCHAR2(30)

*_REPCAT

Lists the interim status of any asynchronous administrative requests and any error messages generated.

SNAME	#VARCHAR2(30)
MASTER	VARCHAR2(1)
STATUS	VARCHAR2(9)
SCHEMA_COMMENT	VARCHAR2(80)
GNAME	#VARCHAR2(30)
FNAME	VARCHAR2(30)
RPC_PROCESSING_DISABLED	VARCHAR2(1)
OWNER	#VARCHAR2(30)

*_REPCATLOG

Lists the interim status of any asynchronous administrative requests and any error messages generated.

ID	#NUMBER
SOURCE	#VARCHAR2(128)
STATUS	VARCHAR2(14)
USERID	VARCHAR2(30)
TIMESTAMP	DATE
ROLE	VARCHAR2(9)
MASTER	#VARCHAR2(128)
SNAME	VARCHAR2(30)
REQUEST	VARCHAR2(29)
ONAME	VARCHAR2(30)
TYPE	VARCHAR2(12)
MESSAGE	VARCHAR2(200)
ERRNUM	NUMBER
GNAME	VARCHAR2(30)

*_REPCOLUMN

Lists replicated columns for a group.

SNAME	#VARCHAR2(30)
ONAME	#VARCHAR2(30)
TYPE	VARCHAR2(8)
CNAME	VARCHAR2(4000)
ID	NUMBER
POS	NUMBER
COMPARE_OLD_ON_DELETE	VARCHAR2(1)
COMPARE_OLD_ON_UPDATE	VARCHAR2(1)
SEND_OLD_ON_DELETE	VARCHAR2(1)
SEND_OLD_ON_UPDATE	VARCHAR2(1)
CTYPE	VARCHAR2(106)
CTYPE_TOID	RAW(16)
CTYPE_OWNER	VARCHAR2(30)
CTYPE_HASHCODE	VARCHAR2(34)
CTYPE_MOD	VARCHAR2(3)
DATA_LENGTH	VARCHAR2(40)
DATA_PRECISION	VARCHAR2(40)
DATA_SCALE	VARCHAR2(40)
NULLABLE	VARCHAR2(1)
CHARACTER_SET_NAME	VARCHAR2(44)
TOP	VARCHAR2(30)
CHAR_LENGTH	NUMBER
CHAR_USED	VARCHAR2(1)

*_REPCOLUMN_GROUP

Lists column groups defined for a table. There is no USER_
REPCOLUMN_GROUP.

SNAME	#VARCHAR2(30)
ONAME	#VARCHAR2(30)
GROUP_NAME	#VARCHAR2(30)
GROUP_COMMENT	VARCHAR2(80)

*_REPCONFLICT

Lists tables with replication conflict resolution methods and
the methods for the tables. There is no USER_REPCON-
FLICT view.

SNAME	#VARCHAR2(30)
ONAME	#VARCHAR2(30)
CONFLICT_TYPE	VARCHAR2(10)
REFERENCE_NAME	#VARCHAR2(30)

*_REPDDL

Lists DDL for replication objects.

LOG_ID	NUMBER
SOURCE	VARCHAR2(128)

ROLE	VARCHAR2(1)
MASTER	VARCHAR2(128)
LINE	NUMBER(38)
TEXT	VARCHAR2(2000)
DDL_NUM	NUMBER(38)

*_REPGENOBJECTS

Lists objects generated to support replication.

SNAME	#VARCHAR2(30)
ONAME	#VARCHAR2(30)
TYPE	VARCHAR2(12)
BASE_SNAME	#VARCHAR2(30)
BASE_ONAME	#VARCHAR2(30)
BASE_TYPE	VARCHAR2(12)
PACKAGE_PREFIX	VARCHAR2(30)
PROCEDURE_PREFIX	VARCHAR2(30)
DISTRIBUTED	VARCHAR2(1)
REASON	VARCHAR2(30)

*_REPGROUP

Lists users who are registered for object group privileges.

SNAME	#VARCHAR2(30)
MASTER	VARCHAR2(1)
STATUS	VARCHAR2(9)
SCHEMA_COMMENT	VARCHAR2(80)
GNAME	#VARCHAR2(30)
FNAME	VARCHAR2(30)
RPC_PROCESSING_DISABLED	VARCHAR2(1)
OWNER	#VARCHAR2(30)

*_REPGROUPED_COLUMN

Lists columns in column groups for each table.

SNAME	#VARCHAR2(30)
ONAME	#VARCHAR2(30)
GROUP_NAME	#VARCHAR2(30)
COLUMN_NAME	#VARCHAR2(30)

*_REPKEY_COLUMNS

Lists information about primary key columns for replicated tables.

SNAME	#VARCHAR2(30)
ONAME	#VARCHAR2(30)
COL	VARCHAR2(4000)

*_REPOBJECT

Lists objects in each replicated object group.

SNAME	VARCHAR2(30)
ONAME	VARCHAR2(30)
TYPE	VARCHAR2(16)
STATUS	VARCHAR2(10)
GENERATION_STATUS	VARCHAR2(9)
ID	NUMBER
OBJECT_COMMENT	VARCHAR2(80)
GNAME	VARCHAR2(30)
MIN_COMMUNICATION	VARCHAR2(1)
REPLICATION_TRIGGER_EXISTS	VARCHAR2(1)
INTERNAL_PACKAGE_EXISTS	VARCHAR2(1)
GROUP_OWNER	VARCHAR2(30)
NESTED_TABLE	VARCHAR2(1)

*_REPPARAMETER_COLUMN

Lists information about columns used to resolve conflicts.

SNAME	#VARCHAR2(30)
ONAME	#VARCHAR2(30)
CONFLICT_TYPE	VARCHAR2(10)
REFERENCE_NAME	#VARCHAR2(30)
SEQUENCE_NO	#NUMBER
METHOD_NAME	#VARCHAR2(80)
FUNCTION_NAME	#VARCHAR2(92)
PRIORITY_GROUP	VARCHAR2(30)
PARAMETER_TABLE_NAME	#VARCHAR2(30)
PARAMETER_COLUMN_NAME	VARCHAR2(4000)
PARAMETER_SEQUENCE_NO	#NUMBER

*_REPPRIORITY

Lists value and priority level of each priority group.

SNAME	#VARCHAR2(30)
PRIORITY_GROUP	#VARCHAR2(30)
PRIORITY	#NUMBER
DATA_TYPE	VARCHAR2(9)
FIXED_DATA_LENGTH	NUMBER(38)
CHAR_VALUE	CHAR(255)
VARCHAR2_VALUE	VARCHAR2(4000)
NUMBER_VALUE	NUMBER
DATE_VALUE	DATE
RAW_VALUE	RAW(2000)
GNAME	#VARCHAR2(30)
NCHAR_VALUE	NCHAR(500)
NVARCHAR2_VALUE	NVARCHAR2(1000)
LARGE_CHAR_VALUE	CHAR(2000)

*_REPPRIORITY_GROUP

Lists priority and site priority groups for a replicated object group.

SNAME	#VARCHAR2(30)
PRIORITY_GROUP	#VARCHAR2(30)
DATA_TYPE	VARCHAR2(9)
FIXED_DATA_LENGTH	NUMBER(38)
PRIORITY_COMMENT	VARCHAR2(80)
GNAME	#VARCHAR2(30)

*_REPPROP

Lists technique used to propagate an object.

SNAME	#VARCHAR2(30)
ONAME	#VARCHAR2(30)
TYPE	VARCHAR2(16)
DBLINK	#VARCHAR2(128)
HOW	VARCHAR2(13)
PROPAGATE_COMMENT	VARCHAR2(80)

*_REPRESOL_STATS_CONTROL

Lists information for statistics collection for conflict resolution.

SNAME	#VARCHAR2(30)
ONAME	#VARCHAR2(30)
CREATED	#DATE
STATUS	VARCHAR2(9)
STATUS_UPDATE_DATE	#DATE
PURGED_DATE	DATE
LAST_PURGE_START_DATE	DATE
LAST_PURGE_END_DATE	DATE

*_REPRESOLUTION

Lists routines used to resolve conflicts for a given schema.

SNAME	#VARCHAR2(30)
ONAME	#VARCHAR2(30)
CONFLICT_TYPE	VARCHAR2(10)
REFERENCE_NAME	#VARCHAR2(30)
SEQUENCE_NO	#NUMBER
METHOD_NAME	#VARCHAR2(80)
FUNCTION_NAME	#VARCHAR2(92)
PRIORITY_GROUP	VARCHAR2(30)
RESOLUTION_COMMENT	VARCHAR2(80)

*_REPRESOLUTION_METHOD

Lists conflict resolution routines.

| CONFLICT_TYPE | VARCHAR2(10) |
| METHOD_NAME | #VARCHAR2(80) |

*_REPRESOLUTION_STATISTICS

Lists information about resolved replication conflicts.

| SNAME | #VARCHAR2(30) |
| ONAME | #VARCHAR2(30) |

CONFLICT_TYPE	VARCHAR2(10)
REFERENCE_NAME	#VARCHAR2(30)
METHOD_NAME	#VARCHAR2(80)
FUNCTION_NAME	VARCHAR2(92)
PRIORITY_GROUP	VARCHAR2(30)
RESOLVED_DATE	#DATE
PRIMARY_KEY_VALUE	#VARCHAR2(2000)

*_REPSITES

Lists members of replicated object groups.

GNAME	#VARCHAR2(30)
DBLINK	#VARCHAR2(128)
MASTERDEF	VARCHAR2(1)
SNAPMASTER	VARCHAR2(1)
MASTER_COMMENT	VARCHAR2(80)
MASTER	VARCHAR2(1)
PROP_UPDATES	NUMBER
MY_DBLINK	VARCHAR2(1)
GROUP_OWNER	#VARCHAR2(30)

Security and auditing

The following views provide information about users, grants, and security policies that implement Oracle's fine-grained access control (FGAC), as well as information about the status of Oracle auditing and audit trails:

ALL_DEF_AUDIT_OPTS

Lists the default auditing options in effect for new objects.

ALT	VARCHAR2(3)
AUD	VARCHAR2(3)
COM	VARCHAR2(3)
DEL	VARCHAR2(3)
GRA	VARCHAR2(3)
IND	VARCHAR2(3)
INS	VARCHAR2(3)
LOC	VARCHAR2(3)
REN	VARCHAR2(3)
SEL	VARCHAR2(3)
UPD	VARCHAR2(3)
REF	VARCHAR2(3)
EXE	VARCHAR2(3)

*_APPLICATION_ROLES

Describes all application roles that have authentication policy roles defined for them. There is no ALL_APPLICATION_ROLES view. New with Oracle9i.

ROLE	#VARCHAR2(30)
SCHEMA	#VARCHAR2(30)
PACKAGE	#VARCHAR2(30)

AUDIT_ACTIONS

Lists the audit codes and descriptions.

| ACTION | #NUMBER |
| NAME | #VARCHAR2(27) |

*_COL_PRIVS

Lists all column grants made in the database.

GRANTEE	#VARCHAR2(30)
OWNER	#VARCHAR2(30)
TABLE_NAME	#VARCHAR2(30)
COLUMN_NAME	#VARCHAR2(30)
GRANTOR	#VARCHAR2(30)
PRIVILEGE	#VARCHAR2(40)
GRANTABLE	VARCHAR2(3)

DBA_AUDIT_EXISTS

Contains audit trail information generated by the EXISTS option of the SQL AUDIT command.

OS_USERNAME	VARCHAR2(255)
USERNAME	VARCHAR2(30)
USERHOST	VARCHAR2(128)
TERMINAL	VARCHAR2(255)
TIMESTAMP	#DATE
OWNER	VARCHAR2(30)
OBJ_NAME	VARCHAR2(128)
ACTION_NAME	VARCHAR2(27)
NEW_OWNER	VARCHAR2(30)
NEW_NAME	VARCHAR2(128)
OBJ_PRIVILEGE	VARCHAR2(16)
SYS_PRIVILEGE	VARCHAR2(40)
GRANTEE	VARCHAR2(30)
SESSIONID	#NUMBER
ENTRYID	#NUMBER
STATEMENTID	#NUMBER
RETURNCODE	#NUMBER
CLIENT_ID	VARCHAR2(64)
SESSION_CPU	NUMBER

DBA_AUDIT_OBJECT

Contains audit trail information for object auditing.

OS_USERNAME	VARCHAR2(255)
USERNAME	VARCHAR2(30)
USERHOST	VARCHAR2(128)

TERMINAL	VARCHAR2(255)
TIMESTAMP	#DATE
OWNER	VARCHAR2(30)
OBJ_NAME	VARCHAR2(128)
ACTION_NAME	VARCHAR2(27)
NEW_OWNER	VARCHAR2(30)
NEW_NAME	VARCHAR2(128)
SES_ACTIONS	VARCHAR2(19)
COMMENT_TEXT	VARCHAR2(4000)
SESSIONID	#NUMBER
ENTRYID	#NUMBER
STATEMENTID	#NUMBER
RETURNCODE	#NUMBER
PRIV_USED	VARCHAR2(40)
CLIENT_ID	VARCHAR2(64)
SESSION_CPU	NUMBER

DBA_AUDIT_SESSION

Contains audit trail information for all connects and disconnects.

OS_USERNAME	VARCHAR2(255)
USERNAME	VARCHAR2(30)
USERHOST	VARCHAR2(128)
TERMINAL	VARCHAR2(255)
TIMESTAMP	#DATE
ACTION_NAME	VARCHAR2(27)
LOGOFF_TIME	DATE
LOGOFF_LREAD	NUMBER
LOGOFF_PREAD	NUMBER
LOGOFF_LWRITE	NUMBER
LOGOFF_DLOCK	VARCHAR2(40)
SESSIONID	#NUMBER
RETURNCODE	#NUMBER
CLIENT_ID	VARCHAR2(64)
SESSION_CPU	NUMBER

DBA_AUDIT_STATEMENT

Contains audit trail information for all audited statements.

OS_USERNAME	VARCHAR2(255)
USERNAME	VARCHAR2(30)
USERHOST	VARCHAR2(128)
TERMINAL	VARCHAR2(255)
TIMESTAMP	#DATE
OWNER	VARCHAR2(30)
OBJ_NAME	VARCHAR2(128)
ACTION_NAME	VARCHAR2(27)
NEW_NAME	VARCHAR2(128)
OBJ_PRIVILEGE	VARCHAR2(16)

SYS_PRIVILEGE	VARCHAR2(40)
ADMIN_OPTION	VARCHAR2(1)
GRANTEE	VARCHAR2(30)
AUDIT_OPTION	VARCHAR2(40)
SES_ACTIONS	VARCHAR2(19)
COMMENT_TEXT	VARCHAR2(4000)
SESSIONID	#NUMBER
ENTRYID	#NUMBER
STATEMENTID	#NUMBER
RETURNCODE	#NUMBER
PRIV_USED	VARCHAR2(40)
CLIENT_ID	VARCHAR2(64)
SESSION_CPU	NUMBER

DBA_AUDIT_TRAIL

Contains all audit trail information.

OS_USERNAME	VARCHAR2(255)
USERNAME	VARCHAR2(30)
USERHOST	VARCHAR2(128)
TERMINAL	VARCHAR2(255)
TIMESTAMP	#DATE
OWNER	VARCHAR2(30)
OBJ_NAME	VARCHAR2(128)
ACTION	#NUMBER
ACTION_NAME	VARCHAR2(27)
NEW_OWNER	VARCHAR2(30)
NEW_NAME	VARCHAR2(128)
OBJ_PRIVILEGE	VARCHAR2(16)
SYS_PRIVILEGE	VARCHAR2(40)
ADMIN_OPTION	VARCHAR2(1)
GRANTEE	VARCHAR2(30)
AUDIT_OPTION	VARCHAR2(40)
SES_ACTIONS	VARCHAR2(19)
LOGOFF_TIME	DATE
LOGOFF_LREAD	NUMBER
LOGOFF_PREAD	NUMBER
LOGOFF_LWRITE	NUMBER
LOGOFF_DLOCK	VARCHAR2(40)
COMMENT_TEXT	VARCHAR2(4000)
SESSIONID	#NUMBER
ENTRYID	#NUMBER
STATEMENTID	#NUMBER
RETURNCODE	#NUMBER
PRIV_USED	VARCHAR2(40)
CLIENT_ID	VARCHAR2(64)
SESSION_CPU	NUMBER

*_GLOBAL_CONTEXT

Lists all the global contexts—sets of application-defined
attributes that can be used to determine access rights available to the instance. There is no USER_GLOBAL_CONTEXT
view. New with Oracle9*i*.

NAMESPACE	#VARCHAR2(30)
SCHEMA	#VARCHAR2(30)
PACKAGE	#VARCHAR2(30)

*_OBJ_AUDIT_OPTS

Lists all object auditing options in effect. There is no ALL_
OBJ_AUDIT_OPTS view.

OWNER	VARCHAR2(30)
OBJECT_NAME	VARCHAR2(30)
OBJECT_TYPE	VARCHAR2(9)
ALT	VARCHAR2(3)
AUD	VARCHAR2(3)
COM	VARCHAR2(3)
DEL	VARCHAR2(3)
GRA	VARCHAR2(3)
IND	VARLHAR2(3)
INS	VARCHAR2(3)
LOC	VARCHAR2(3)
REN	VARCHAR2(3)
SEL	VARCHAR2(3)
UPD	VARCHAR2(3)
REF	VARCHAR2(3)
EXE	VARCHAR2(3)
CRE	VARCHAR2(3)
REA	VARCHAR2(3)
WRI	VARCHAR2(3)

*_POLICIES

Lists information about policies. New with Oracle9*i*.

OBJECT_OWNER	VARCHAR2(30)
OBJECT_NAME	VARCHAR2(30)
POLICY_GROUP	VARCHAR2(30)

POLICY_NAME	VARCHAR2(30)
PF_OWNER	VARCHAR2(30)
PACKAGE	VARCHAR2(30)
FUNCTION	VARCHAR2(30)
SEL	VARCHAR2(3)
INS	VARCHAR2(3)
UPD	VARCHAR2(3)
DEL	VARCHAR2(3)
CHK_OPTION	VARCHAR2(3)
ENABLE	VARCHAR2(3)
STATIC_POLICY	VARCHAR2(3)

*_POLICY_CONTEXTS

Lists policies and their associated contexts. New with Oracle9i.

OBJECT_OWNER	VARCHAR2(30)
OBJECT_NAME	VARCHAR2(30)
NAMESPACE	VARCHAR2(30)
ATTRIBUTE	VARCHAR2(30)

*_POLICY_GROUPS

Lists the various groups for the different security policies. New with Oracle9i.

OBJECT_OWNER	VARCHAR2(30)
OBJECT_NAME	VARCHAR2(30)
POLICY_GROUP	VARCHAR2(30)

*_PRIV_AUDIT_OPTS

Lists all system privilege auditing options in effect.

USER_NAME	VARCHAR2(30)
PROXY_NAME	VARCHAR2(30)
PRIVILEGE	#VARCHAR2(40)
SUCCESS	VARCHAR2(10)
FAILURE	VARCHAR2(10)

*_PROFILES

Lists all defined profiles.

PROFILE	#VARCHAR2(30)
RESOURCE_NAME	#VARCHAR2(32)
RESOURCE_TYPE	VARCHAR2(8)
LIMIT	VARCHAR2(40)

RESOURCE_COST

Shows the assigned cost of each resource for composite limits.

| RESOURCE_NAME | #VARCHAR2(32) |
| UNIT_COST | #NUMBER |

RESOURCE_MAP

Maps profile resource numbers to resource names.

RESOURCE#	#NUMBER
TYPE#	#NUMBER
NAME	#VARCHAR2(32)

*_ROLE_PRIVS

Lists all roles granted to users and to other roles.

GRANTEE	VARCHAR2(30)
GRANTED_ROLE	#VARCHAR2(30)
ADMIN_OPTION	VARCHAR2(3)
DEFAULT_ROLE	VARCHAR2(3)

ROLE_ROLE_PRIVS

Lists roles granted to other roles.

GRANTEE	VARCHAR2(30)
GRANTED_ROLE	#VARCHAR2(30)
ADMIN OPTION	VARCHAR2(3)
DEFAULT_ROLE	VARCHAR2(3)

NOTE

The ROLE_ROLE_PRIVS view is a subset of *_ROLE_PRIVS.

ROLE_SYS_PRIVS

Lists only system privileges granted to roles.

GRANTEE	#VARCHAR2(30)
PRIVILEGE	#VARCHAR2(40)
ADMIN_OPTION	VARCHAR2(3)

NOTE

The ROLE_SYS_PRIVS view is a subset of *_SYS_PRIVS.

ROLE_TAB_PRIVS

Lists table grants granted to roles.

GRANTEE	#VARCHAR2(30)
OWNER	#VARCHAR2(30)
TABLE_NAME	#VARCHAR2(30)
GRANTOR	#VARCHAR2(30)
PRIVILEGE	#VARCHAR2(40)
GRANTABLE	VARCHAR2(3)
HIERARCHY	VARCHAR2(3)

*_ROLES

Lists all roles.

ROLE	#VARCHAR2(30)
PASSWORD_REQUIRED	VARCHAR2(8)

SESSION_PRIVS

Shows which system privileges are active for the current session.

PRIVILEGE	#VARCHAR2(40)

SESSION_ROLES

Shows which roles are active for the current session.

ROLE	#VARCHAR2(30)

STMT_AUDIT_OPTION_MAP

Lists the valid SQL statements that can be specified for statement auditing.

OPTION#	#NUMBER
NAME	#VARCHAR2(40)
PROPERTY	#NUMBER

*_STMT_AUDIT_OPTS

Lists all statement auditing options in effect.

USER_NAME	VARCHAR2(30)
PROXY_NAME	VARCHAR2(30)
AUDIT_OPTION	#VARCHAR2(40)
SUCCESS	VARCHAR2(10)
FAILURE	VARCHAR2(10)

*_SYS_PRIVS

Shows which system privileges have been assigned to which users.

GRANTEE	#VARCHAR2(30)
PRIVILEGE	#VARCHAR2(40)
ADMIN_OPTION	VARCHAR2(3)

SYSTEM_PRIVILEGE_MAP

Lists the valid system privileges that can be specified for system privilege auditing.

PRIVILEGE	#NUMBER
NAME	#VARCHAR2(40)
PROPERTY	#NUMBER

*_TAB_PRIVS

Shows all object privileges.

GRANTEE	#VARCHAR2(30)
OWNER	#VARCHAR2(30)
TABLE_NAME	#VARCHAR2(30)
GRANTOR	#VARCHAR2(30)
PRIVILEGE	#VARCHAR2(40)
GRANTABLE	VARCHAR2(3)
HIERARCHY	VARCHAR2(3)

NOTE

The name of the *_TAB_PRIVS view is misleading; it actually includes not only tables but also views, sequences, packages, procedures, and functions.

TABLE_PRIVILEGE_MAP

Lists the valid object audit options that can be specified for schema object auditing.

PRIVILEGE	#NUMBER
NAME	#VARCHAR2(40)

USER_PASSWORD_LIMITS

Shows the password limits in effect for the current session.

RESOURCE_NAME	#VARCHAR2(32)
LIMIT	VARCHAR2(40)

*_USERS

Lists all users and their basic database-related characteristics. Although the ALL_USERS view is available, it contains

only the USERNAME, USER_ID, and CREATED columns.
There is no USER_USERS view.

```
USERNAME                       #VARCHAR2(30)
USER_ID                        #NUMBER
PASSWORD                        VARCHAR2(30)
ACCOUNT_STATUS                 #VARCHAR2(32)
LOCK_DATE                       DATE
EXPIRY_DATE                     DATE
DEFAULT_TABLESPACE             #VARCHAR2(30)
TEMPORARY_TABLESPACE           #VARCHAR2(30)
CREATED                        #DATE
PROFILE                        #VARCHAR2(30)
INITIAL_RSRC_CONSUMER_GROUP     VARCHAR2(30)
EXTERNAL_NAME                   VARCHAR2(4000)
```

NOTE

Because Oracle (by default) assigns the SYSTEM tablespace as a user's TEMPORARY and DEFAULT tablespaces, the following query lets the DBA identify those accounts whose tablespace assignments should be changed:

```
SELECT username
FROM dba_users
WHERE TEMPORARY_TABLESPACE = 'SYSTEM'
OR DEFAULT_TABLESPACE = 'SYSTEM';
```

Server information

The following views provide information about a variety of database parameters and other information:

DBA_UNDO_EXTENTS

Lists the commit time of each extent in the UNDO tablespace. New with Oracle9i.

```
OWNER                          CHAR(3)
SEGMENT_NAME                   #VARCHAR2(30)
TABLESPACE_NAME                #VARCHAR2(30)
EXTENT_ID                       NUMBER
FILE_ID                        #NUMBER
BLOCK_ID                        NUMBER
BYTES                           NUMBER
BLOCKS                          NUMBER
RELATIVE_FNO                    NUMBER
```

COMMIT_JTIME	NUMBER
COMMIT_WTIME	VARCHAR2(20)
STATUS	VARCHAR2(9)

NLS_DATABASE_PARAMETERS

Shows the National Language Support (NLS) parameters in effect at the database level.

| PARAMETER | #VARCHAR2(30) |
| VALUE | VARCHAR2(40) |

NLS_INSTANCE_PARAMETERS

Shows the NLS parameters in effect at the instance level.

| PARAMETER | #VARCHAR2(30) |
| VALUE | VARCHAR2(40) |

NLS_SESSION_PARAMETERS

Shows the NLS parameters in effect at the session level.

| PARAMETER | #VARCIIAR2(30) |
| VALUE | VARCHAR2(40) |

PRODUCT_COMPONENT_VERSION

Shows the current release level of all installed Oracle options.

PRODUCT	VARCHAR2(64)
VERSION	VARCHAR2(64)
STATUS	VARCHAR2(64)

*_PROXIES

Lists information about all proxy connections in the system. There is no ALL_ PROXIES view. New with Oracle9i.

PROXY	#VARCHAR2(30)
CLIENT	#VARCHAR2(30)
CREDENTIAL	VARCHAR2(18)
TYPE	VARCHAR2(5)
VERSION	VARCHAR2(1)
AUTHORIZATION_CONSTRAINT	VARCHAR2(35)
ROLE	VARCHAR2(30)

*_RESUMABLE

Lists all RESUMABLE statements. When the database runs out of space, these statements allows the DBA to suspend an operation, add more space, and then resume the operation. There is no ALL_RESUMABLE view. New with Oracle9i.

USER_ID	NUMBER
SESSION_ID	NUMBER
INSTANCE_ID	NUMBER
COORD_INSTANCE_ID	NUMBER

COORD_SESSION_ID	NUMBER
STATUS	VARCHAR2(9)
TIMEOUT	NUMBER
START_TIME	VARCHAR2(20)
SUSPEND_TIME	VARCHAR2(20)
RESUME_TIME	VARCHAR2(20)
NAME	VARCHAR2(4000)
SQL_TEXT	VARCHAR2(1000)
ERROR_NUMBER	NUMBER
ERROR_PARAMETER1	VARCHAR2(80)
ERROR_PARAMETER2	VARCHAR2(80)
ERROR_PARAMETER3	VARCHAR2(80)
ERROR_PARAMETER4	VARCHAR2(80)
ERROR_PARAMETER5	VARCHAR2(80)
ERROR_MSG	VARCHAR2(4000)

*_SEQUENCES

Lists all sequences in the database.

SEQUENCE_OWNER	#VARCHAR2(30)
SEQUENCE_NAME	#VARCHAR2(30)
MIN_VALUE	NUMBER
MAX_VALUE	NUMBER
INCREMENT_BY	#NUMBER
CYCLE_FLAG	VARCHAR2(1)
ORDER_FLAG	VARCHAR2(1)
CACHE_SIZE	#NUMBER
LAST_NUMBER	#NUMBER

SM$VERSION

Shows the Oracle version level for use by Server Manager.

VERSION_TEXT	CHAR(9)
VERSION_NUMBER	NUMBER
CREATED	DATE

*_SYNONYMS

Lists all synonyms in the database.

OWNER	#VARCHAR2(30)
SYNONYM_NAME	#VARCHAR2(30)
TABLE_OWNER	VARCHAR2(30)
TABLE_NAME	#VARCHAR2(30)
DB_LINK	VARCHAR2(128)

SQLJ

SQLJ is used to embed static SQL statements into a Java™ program. SQLJ statements access SQLJ objects, which are composite data structures related to the SQLJ statements.

SQLJ objects are stored in the Oracle database and are described through the following views:

*_SQLJ_TYPE_ATTRS

Lists the attributes associated with each SQLJ object type. New with Oracle9*i*.

OWNER	VARCHAR2(30)
TYPE_NAME	#VARCHAR2(30)
ATTR_NAME	#VARCHAR2(30)
EXTERNAL_ATTR_NAME	VARCHAR2(4000)
ATTR_TYPE_MOD	VARCHAR2(7)
ATTR_TYPE_OWNER	VARCHAR2(30)
ATTR_TYPE_NAME	VARCHAR2(30)
LENGTH	NUMBER
PRECISION	NUMBER
SCALE	NUMBER
CHARACTER_SET_NAME	VARCHAR2(44)
ATTR_NO	#NUMBER
INHERITED	VARCHAR2(3)

*_SQLJ_TYPE_METHODS

Describes the methods associated with each SQLJ object type. New with Oracle9*i*.

OWNER	#VARCHAR2(30)
TYPE_NAME	#VARCHAR2(30)
METHOD_NAME	#VARCHAR2(30)
EXTERNAL_VAR_NAME	VARCHAR2(4000)
METHOD_NO	#NUMBER
METHOD_TYPE	VARCHAR2(6)
PARAMETERS	#NUMBER
RESULTS	#NUMBER
FINAL	VARCHAR2(3)
INSTANTIABLE	VARCHAR2(3)
OVERRIDING	VARCHAR2(3)
INHERITED	VARCHAR2(3)

*_SQLJ_TYPES

Describes the SQLJ object types. New with Oracle9*i*.

OWNER	VARCHAR2(30)
TYPE_NAME	#VARCHAR2(30)
TYPE_OID	#RAW(16)
EXTERNAL_NAME	VARCHAR2(4000)
USING	VARCHAR2(21)
TYPECODE	VARCHAR2(30)
ATTRIBUTES	NUMBER
METHODS	NUMBER
PREDEFINED	VARCHAR2(3)

INCOMPLETE	VARCHAR2(3)
FINAL	VARCHAR2(3)
INSTANTIABLE	VARCHAR2(3)
SUPERTYPE_OWNER	VARCHAR2(30)
SUPERTYPE_NAME	VARCHAR2(30)
LOCAL_ATTRIBUTES	NUMBER
LOCAL_METHODS	NUMBER

Storage

The following views provide information about internal storage in the database, including datafiles, tablespaces, free extents, used extents, and segments:

DBA_DATA_FILES

Lists all datafiles comprising the database.

FILE_NAME	VARCHAR2(513)
FILE_ID	NUMBER
TABLESPACE_NAME	VARCHAR2(30)
BYTES	NUMBER
BLOCKS	NUMBER
STATUS	VARCHAR2(9)
RELATIVE_FNO	NUMBER
AUTOEXTENSIBLE	VARCHAR2(3)
MAXBYTES	NUMBER
MAXBLOCKS	NUMBER
INCREMENT_BY	NUMBER
USER_BYTES	NUMBER
USER_BLOCKS	NUMBER

NOTE

DBAs often need to know what tablespaces have AUTOEX-TEND enabled and which datafile(s) will be affected when a tablespace needs to extend. The following query provides this information:

```
SELECT tablespace_name,file_name
FROM dba_data_files
WHERE autoextensible = 'Y';
```

DBA_FREE_SPACE

Lists every free extent.

TABLESPACE_NAME	VARCHAR2(30)
FILE_ID	NUMBER
BLOCK_ID	NUMBER

BYTES	NUMBER
BLOCKS	NUMBER
RELATIVE_FNO	NUMBER

NOTE

This view, combined with *_EXTENTS, should account for all storage in *_DATA_FILES. You can find the total amount of free space in each tablespace with this query:

```
SELECT tablespace_name, sum(bytes)
FROM dba_free_space
GROUP BY tablespace_name;
```

DBA_ROLLBACK_SEGS

Lists all rollback segments.

SEGMENT_NAME	#VARCHAR2(30)
OWNER	VARCHAR2(6)
TABLESPACE_NAME	#VARCHAR2(30)
SEGMENT_ID	#NUMBER
FILE_ID	#NUMBER
BLOCK_ID	#NUMBER
INITIAL_EXTENT	NUMBER
NEXT_EXTENT	NUMBER
MIN_EXTENTS	#NUMBER
MAX_EXTENTS	#NUMBER
PCT_INCREASE	NUMBER
STATUS	VARCHAR2(16)
INSTANCE_NUM	VARCHAR2(40)
RELATIVE_FNO	#NUMBER

*_EXTENTS

Lists every allocated extent for every segment.

OWNER	VARCHAR2(30)
SEGMENT_NAME	VARCHAR2(81)
PARTITION_NAME	VARCHAR2(30)
SEGMENT_TYPE	VARCHAR2(18)
TABLESPACE_NAME	VARCHAR2(30)
EXTENT_ID	NUMBER
FILE_ID	NUMBER
BLOCK_ID	NUMBER
BYTES	NUMBER
BLOCKS	NUMBER
RELATIVE_FNO	NUMBER

*_FREE_SPACE_COALESCED

Lists every extent that is at the start of a block of free extents.

TABLESPACE_NAME	VARCHAR2(30)
TOTAL_EXTENTS	NUMBER
EXTENTS_COALESCED	NUMBER
PERCENT_EXTENTS_COALESCED	NUMBER
TOTAL_BYTES	NUMBER
BYTES_COALESCED	NUMBER
TOTAL_BLOCKS	NUMBER
BLOCKS_COALESCED	NUMBER
PERCENT_BLOCKS_COALESCED	NUMBER

*_SEGMENTS

Lists all segments.

OWNER	VARCHAR2(30)
SEGMENT_NAME	VARCHAR2(81)
PARTITION_NAME	VARCHAR2(30)
SEGMENT_TYPE	VARCHAR2(18)
TABLESPACE_NAME	VARCHAR2(30)
HEADER_FILE	NUMBER
HEADER_BLOCK	NUMBER
BYTES	NUMBER
BLOCKS	NUMBER
EXTENTS	NUMBER
INITIAL_EXTENT	NUMBER
NEXT_EXTENT	NUMBER
MIN_EXTENTS	NUMBER
MAX_EXTENTS	NUMBER
PCT_INCREASE	NUMBER
FREELISTS	NUMBER
FREELIST_GROUPS	NUMBER
RELATIVE_FNO	NUMBER
BUFFER_POOL	VARCHAR2(7)

> **NOTE**
>
> You can determine the number of bytes or database blocks occupied by an object by specifying the following query:
>
> ```
> SELECT bytes, blocks
> FROM dba_segments
> WHERE segment_name = 'segment_name'
> ```

*_TABLESPACES

Lists all tablespaces in the database.

TABLESPACE_NAME	#VARCHAR2(30)
BLOCK_SIZE	#NUMBER
INITIAL_EXTENT	NUMBER
NEXT_EXTENT	NUMBER
MIN_EXTENTS	#NUMBER
MAX_EXTENTS	NUMBER
PCT_INCREASE	NUMBER
MIN_EXTLEN	NUMBER
STATUS	VARCHAR2(9)
CONTENTS	VARCHAR2(9)
LOGGING	VARCHAR2(9)
FORCE_LOGGING	VARCHAR2(3)
EXTENT_MANAGEMENT	VARCHAR2(10)
ALLOCATION_TYPE	VARCHAR2(9)
PLUGGED_IN	VARCHAR2(3)
SEGMENT_SPACE_MANAGEMENT	VARCHAR2(6)

*_TS_QUOTAS

Shows the granted quota and used storage in tablespaces by user.

TABLESPACE_NAME	#VARCHAR2(30)
USERNAME	#VARCHAR2(30)
BYTES	NUMBER
MAX_BYTES	NUMBER
BLOCKS	#NUMBER
MAX_BLOCKS	NUMBER

Tables, columns, and views

Tables are the most important building blocks of an Oracle database. These views provide information about tables, columns, clusters, and views:

*_ALL_TABLES

Lists all object and relational tables.

OWNER	VARCHAR2(30)
TABLE_NAME	VARCHAR2(30)
TABLESPACE_NAME	VARCHAR2(30)
CLUSTER_NAME	VARCHAR2(30)
IOT_NAME	VARCHAR2(30)
PCT_FREE	NUMBER
PCT_USED	NUMBER
INI_TRANS	NUMBER
MAX_TRANS	NUMBER
INITIAL_EXTENT	NUMBER
NEXT_EXTENT	NUMBER
MIN_EXTENTS	NUMBER
MAX_EXTENTS	NUMBER
PCT_INCREASE	NUMBER
FREELISTS	NUMBER
FREELIST_GROUPS	NUMBER
LOGGING	VARCHAR2(3)
BACKED_UP	VARCHAR2(1)
NUM_ROWS	NUMBER
BLOCKS	NUMBER
EMPTY_BLOCKS	NUMBER
AVG_SPACE	NUMBER
CHAIN_CNT	NUMBER
AVG_ROW_LEN	NUMBER
AVG_SPACE_FREELIST_BLOCKS	NUMBER
NUM_FREELIST_BLOCKS	NUMBER
DEGREE	VARCHAR2(10)
INSTANCES	VARCHAR2(10)
CACHE	VARCHAR2(5)
TABLE_LOCK	VARCHAR2(8)
SAMPLE_SIZE	NUMBER
LAST_ANALYZED	DATE
PARTITIONED	VARCHAR2(3)
IOT_TYPE	VARCHAR2(12)
OBJECT_ID_TYPE	VARCHAR2(16)
TABLE_TYPE_OWNER	VARCHAR2(30)
TABLE_TYPE	VARCHAR2(30)
TEMPORARY	VARCHAR2(1)
SECONDARY	VARCHAR2(1)
NESTED	VARCHAR2(3)
BUFFER_POOL	VARCHAR2(7)
ROW_MOVEMENT	VARCHAR2(8)
GLOBAL_STATS	VARCHAR2(3)
USER_STATS	VARCHAR2(3)
DURATION	VARCHAR2(15)
SKIP_CORRUPT	VARCHAR2(8)
MONITORING	VARCHAR2(3)
CLUSTER_OWNER	VARCHAR2(30)
DEPENDENCIES	VARCHAR2(8)

*_CLU_COLUMNS

Lists all cluster keys.

CLUSTER_NAME	#VARCHAR2(30)
CLU_COLUMN_NAME	#VARCHAR2(30)
TABLE_NAME	#VARCHAR2(30)
TAB_COLUMN_NAME	VARCHAR2(4000)

*_CLUSTER_HASH_EXPRESSIONS

Lists the hash values used for the optional cluster hash indexes.

OWNER	#VARCHAR2(30)
CLUSTER_NAME	#VARCHAR2(30)
HASH_EXPRESSION	LONG

*_CLUSTERS

Lists all clusters in the database.

OWNER	#VARCHAR2(30)
CLUSTER_NAME	#VARCHAR2(30)
TABLESPACE_NAME	#VARCHAR2(30)
PCT_FREE	NUMBER
PCT_USED	NUMBER
KEY_SIZE	NUMBER
INI_TRANS	#NUMBER
MAX_TRANS	#NUMBER
INITIAL_EXTENT	NUMBER
NEXT_EXTENT	NUMBER
MIN_EXTENTS	#NUMBER
MAX_EXTENTS	#NUMBER
PCT_INCREASE	NUMBER
FREELISTS	NUMBER
FREELIST_GROUPS	NUMBER
AVG_BLOCKS_PER_KEY	NUMBER
CLUSTER_TYPE	VARCHAR2(5)
FUNCTION	VARCHAR2(15)
HASHKEYS	NUMBER
DEGREE	VARCHAR2(10)
INSTANCES	VARCHAR2(10)
CACHE	VARCHAR2(5)
BUFFER_POOL	VARCHAR2(7)

| SINGLE_TABLE | VARCHAR2(5) |
| DEPENDENCIES | VARCHAR2(8) |

*_COL_COMMENTS

Shows comments on all table and view columns.

OWNER	#VARCHAR2(30)
TABLE_NAME	#VARCHAR2(30)
COLUMN_NAME	#VARCHAR2(30)
COMMENTS	VARCHAR2(4000)

*_EXTERNAL_LOCATIONS

Lists the sources for the external tables.

OWNER	#VARCHAR2(30)
TABLE_NAME	#VARCHAR2(30)
LOCATION	VARCHAR2(4000)
DIRECTORY_OWNER	CHAR(3)
DIRECTORY_NAME	VARCHAR2(30)

*_EXTERNAL_TABLES

Describes the attributes of external tables.

OWNER	#VARCHAR2(30)
TABLE_NAME	#VARCHAR2(30)
TYPE_OWNER	CHAR(3)
TYPE_NAME	#VARCHAR2(30)
DEFAULT_DIRECTORY_OWNER	CHAR(3)
DEFAULT_DIRECTORY_NAME	#VARCHAR2(30)
REJECT_LIMIT	VARCHAR2(40)
ACCESS_TYPE	VARCHAR2(7)
ACCESS_PARAMETERS	VARCHAR2(4000)

*_TAB_COL_STATISTICS

Contains column information about analyzed columns.

OWNER	#VARCHAR2(30)
TABLE_NAME	#VARCHAR2(30)
COLUMN_NAME	#VARCHAR2(30)
NUM_DISTINCT	NUMBER
LOW_VALUE	RAW(32)
HIGH_VALUE	RAW(32)
DENSITY	NUMBER
NUM_NULLS	NUMBER
NUM_BUCKETS	NUMBER
LAST_ANALYZED	DATE
SAMPLE_SIZE	NUMBER
GLOBAL_STATS	VARCHAR2(3)
USER_STATS	VARCHAR2(3)
AVG_COL_LEN	NUMBER

The *_TAB_COL_STATISTICS view only contains rows for tables that have been analyzed.

*_TAB_COLUMNS

Shows all table and view columns.

Column	Type
OWNER	#VARCHAR2(30)
TABLE_NAME	#VARCHAR2(30)
COLUMN_NAME	#VARCHAR2(30)
DATA_TYPE	VARCHAR2(106)
DATA_TYPE_MOD	VARCHAR2(3)
DATA_TYPE_OWNER	VARCHAR2(30)
DATA_LENGTH	#NUMBER
DATA_PRECISION	NUMBER
DATA_SCALE	NUMBER
NULLABLE	VARCHAR2(1)
COLUMN_ID	NUMBER
DEFAULT_LENGTH	NUMBER
DATA_DEFAULT	LONG
NUM_DISTINCT	NUMBER
LOW_VALUE	RAW(32)
HIGH_VALUE	RAW(32)
DENSITY	NUMBER
NUM_NULLS	NUMBER
NUM_BUCKETS	NUMBER
LAST_ANALYZED	DATE
SAMPLE_SIZE	NUMBER
CHARACTER_SET_NAME	VARCHAR2(44)
CHAR_COL_DECL_LENGTH	NUMBER
GLOBAL_STATS	VARCHAR2(3)
USER_STATS	VARCHAR2(3)
AVG_COL_LEN	NUMBER
CHAR_LENGTH	NUMBER
CHAR_USED	VARCHAR2(1)
V80_FMT_IMAGE	VARCHAR2(3)
DATA_UPGRADED	VARCHAR2(3)

*_TAB_COMMENTS

Shows all comments on tables and views.

OWNER	#VARCHAR2(30)
TABLE_NAME	#VARCHAR2(30)
TABLE_TYPE	VARCHAR2(11)
COMMENTS	VARCHAR2(4000)

*_TAB_HISTOGRAMS

Shows all table histograms.

OWNER	VARCHAR2(30)
TABLE_NAME	VARCHAR2(30)
COLUMN_NAME	VARCHAR2(4000)
ENDPOINT_NUMBER	NUMBER
ENDPOINT_VALUE	NUMBER
ENDPOINT_ACTUAL_VALUE	VARCHAR2(1000)

*_TABLES

Shows all relational tables.

OWNER	#VARCHAR2(30)
TABLE_NAME	#VARCHAR2(30)
TABLESPACE_NAME	VARCHAR2(30)
CLUSTER_NAME	VARCHAR2(30)
IOT_NAME	VARCHAR2(30)
PCT_FREE	NUMBER
PCT_USED	NUMBER
INI_TRANS	NUMBER
MAX_TRANS	NUMBER
INITIAL_EXTENT	NUMBER

NEXT_EXTENT	NUMBER
MIN_EXTENTS	NUMBER
MAX_EXTENTS	NUMBER
PCT_INCREASE	NUMBER
FREELISTS	NUMBER
FREELIST_GROUPS	NUMBER
LOGGING	VARCHAR2(3)
BACKED_UP	VARCHAR2(1)
NUM_ROWS	NUMBER
BLOCKS	NUMBER
EMPTY_BLOCKS	NUMBER
AVG_SPACE	NUMBER
CHAIN_CNT	NUMBER
AVG_ROW_LEN	NUMBER
AVG_SPACE_FREELIST_BLOCKS	NUMBER
NUM_FREELIST_BLOCKS	NUMBER
DEGREE	VARCHAR2(10)
INSTANCES	VARCHAR2(10)
CACHE	VARCHAR2(5)
TABLE_LOCK	VARCHAR2(8)
SAMPLE_SIZE	NUMBER
LAST_ANALYZED	DATE
PARTITIONED	VARCHAR2(3)
IOT_TYPE	VARCHAR2(12)
TEMPORARY	VARCHAR2(1)
SECONDARY	VARCHAR2(1)
NESTED	VARCHAR2(3)
BUFFER_POOL	VARCHAR2(7)
ROW_MOVEMENT	VARCHAR2(8)
GLOBAL_STATS	VARCHAR2(3)
USER_STATS	VARCHAR2(3)
DURATION	VARCHAR2(15)
SKIP_CORRUPT	VARCHAR2(8)
MONITORING	VARCHAR2(3)
CLUSTER_OWNER	VARCHAR2(30)
DEPENDENCIES	VARCHAR2(8)

*_UPDATABLE_COLUMNS

Lists columns that can be updated in views with joins.

OWNER	#VARCHAR2(30)
TABLE_NAME	#VARCHAR2(30)
COLUMN_NAME	#VARCHAR2(30)
UPDATABLE	VARCHAR2(3)
INSERTABLE	VARCHAR2(3)
DELETABLE	VARCHAR2(3)

*_VIEWS

Shows all views.

OWNER	#VARCHAR2(30)
VIEW_NAME	#VARCHAR2(30)
TEXT_LENGTH	NUMBER
TEXT	LONG
TYPE_TEXT_LENGTH	NUMBER
TYPE_TEXT	VARCHAR2(4000)
OID_TEXT_LENGTH	NUMBER
OID_TEXT	VARCHAR2(4000)
VIEW_TYPE_OWNER	VARCHAR2(30)
VIEW_TYPE	VARCHAR2(30)
SUPERVIEW_NAME	VARCHAR2(30)

Other Static Data Dictionary Views

The static data dictionary views listed in the following sections contain important information about the structure of the database. However, unlike the views described in previous sections, these views are normally not referenced directly.

Export/Import

The following views provide information to the Export and Import utilities:

    *_EXP_FILES
    *_EXP_OBJECTS
    *_EXP_VERSION

Gateways

The following views provide information needed to support foreign data sources (FDSs) or data gateways. Note that in these view names, "HS" stands for Heterogeneous Services, Oracle's name for its gateway technologies:

    HS_ALL_CAPS
    HS_ALL_DD
    HS_ALL_INITS
    HS_BASE_CAPS
    HS_BASE_DD
    HS_CLASS_CAPS
    HS_CLASS_DD

```
HS_CLASS_INIT
HS_EXTERNAL_OBJECT_PRIVILEGES
HS_EXTERNAL_OBJECTS
HS_EXTERNAL_USER_PRIVILEGES
HS_FDS_CLASS
HS_FDS_INST
HS_INST_CAPS
HS_INST_DD
HS_INST_INIT
```

Oracle Parallel Server/Real Application Clusters

The following views provide information about the status of
the Oracle Parallel Server/Real Application Clusters environment. Note, however, that standard use of Real Application
Clusters does not involve these type of locks and pings:

```
FILE_LOCK
FILE_PING
```

Remote procedure calls

The following views provide information about the status of
remote procedure calls (RPCs):

```
DEFCALL
DEFDEFAULTDEST
DEFERRCOUNT
DEFERROR
DEFLOB
DEFPROPAGATOR
DEFSCHEDULE
DEFTRAN
DEFTRANDEST
ORA_KGLR7_DB_LINKS
ORA_KGLR7_DEPENDENCIES
ORA_KGLR7_IDL_CHAR
ORA_KGLR7_IDL_SB4
ORA_KGLR7_IDL_UB1
ORA_KGLR7_IDL_UB2
```

Snapshots

The following views provide information about snapshots or their replacement, materialized views (MVIEWS):

```
*_RCHILD
*_REFRESH
*_REFRESH_CHILDREN
*_REGISTERED_SNAPSHOTS
*_REGISTERED_MVIEWS
*_RGROUP
*_SNAPSHOT_LOGS/MVIEW_LOGS
*_SNAPSHOT_REFRESH_TIMES
*_MVIEW_REFRESH_TIMES
*_SNAPSHOTS/MVIEWS
DBA_REGISTERED_SNAPSHOT_GROUPS
DBA_SNAPSHOT_LOG_FILTER_COLS
```

SQL*Loader direct path

The following views provide information used by the SQL*Loader direct path option:

```
LOADER_CONSTRAINT_INFO
LOADER_FILE_TS
LOADER_PARAM_INFO
LOADER_PART_INFO
LOADER_TAB_INFO
LOADER_TRIGGER_INFO
```

Tablespace point-in-time recovery

The following views provide information required for tablespace point-in-time recovery (PITR):

```
STRADDLING_RS_OBJECTS
TS_PITR_CHECK
TS_PITR_OBJECTS_TO_BE_DROPPED
```

Dynamic Data Dictionary Views

The dynamic performance views (the V$ views) mainly provide information about the Oracle instance, as well as information that the instance maintains about the database. The views in this category are considered dynamic, because in general, their contents change based upon how the instance is performing. The contents of these views are representative of the total instance or cluster workload, rather than any one specific SQL statement.

Availability of Dynamic Data Dictionary Views

Specific dynamic performance views are available based on the status of the instance, as follows:

- Those views that provide information specifically about the instance (e.g., V$PARAMETER) are available immediately once the instance is started.

- Those views that provide information stored in the control files are available once the database has been mounted (as noted in the view description).

- Those views that provide information about how the kernel is processing SQL statements are available once the database has been opened (as noted in the view description).

How Dynamic Data Dictionary Views Are Built

Unlike the static data dictionary views, which are views on existing tables, the dynamic performance data dictionary views are views on a set of tables that do not physically exist in the database; instead they are actually views on X$ tables, which in turn are representations of internal memory structures in the Oracle instance. Views are constructed as follows:

- SYS.V_$DATABASE is a view on the fixed view V$DATABASE. A *fixed view* is one that cannot be altered or removed by the DBA.
- The fixed view V$DATABASE is a view on GV$DATABASE that extracts information for the current instance.
- GV$DATABSE is a public synonym for the view SYS.GV_ $DATABASE.
- SYS.GV_$DATABASE is a view on the fixed view GV$DATABASE.
- The fixed view GV$DATABASE is a view on the virtual table (a memory structure) X$KCCDI.

NOTE

The exact specification of how the V$ views are built is maintained within the Oracle kernel. The view V$FIXED_VIEW_DEFINITION defines all V$ views as views based upon the X$ tables.

Understanding how these views are built is important to understanding how they work. Initially defined within the Oracle kernel, these "hardcoded" V$ views are accessible once the instance has been started or once the database has been mounted. Once the database is opened, the normal SQL processing takes over, and the public synonyms referencing the views are used. With public synonyms, the same name is available whether you are connected INTERNAL before the database is opened or are connected as a user with DBA privileges after the database is opened. Note that non-DBA users do not normally have access to the V$ views, but DBAs can grant this access on an individual view basis.

A few V$ views are true views, based on X$ or other V$ tables; these are not available until the database is opened.

Global Dynamic Data Dictionary Views (GV$ Views)

Beginning with Oracle8, the dynamic performance data dictionary views (V$ views) were augmented with a complementary set of global dynamic performance data dictionary views (GV$ views). The V$ views provide information about the instance to which you are connected and its management of the database. The GV$ views provide the same information for all other instances that have the same database mounted, and are primarily of interest in a Real Applications Cluster or Oracle Parallel Server environment.

The global dynamic performance data dictionary views add the column INST_ID to their names, which allows you to identify the instance for which information is being provided. Because the GV$ views are the same as the V$ views presented in this book except for the addition of INST_ID (and in the interest of space and clarity), these views are not explicitly listed here.

Commonly Used Dynamic Data Dictionary Views

The following sections summarize the Oracle dynamic performance data dictionary views. Because related views are sometimes used together, I have grouped them in the following way:

Advanced Queuing
Configuration
Data dictionary cache
Database
Instance
Locks and latches
Multi-Threaded Server/Shared Servers
Oracle Parallel Server/Real Application Clusters
Parallel Query

Recovery
Replication
Resource allocation
Session
System Global Area
SQL
SQL*Loader direct path
System environment

Some additional views exist in Oracle (and more are added in each version) that are intended primarily for internal use by the Oracle kernel. Because these views are not likely to be used by DBAs or developers (and, again, in the interest of space and clarity), these views are not included here.

Advanced Queuing

This view provides throughput statistics for the Advanced Queuing facility:

V$AQ

Provides message statistics for each of the Advanced Queuing message queues. Available after database is opened.

QID	NUMBER
WAITING	NUMBER
READY	NUMBER
EXPIRED	NUMBER
TOTAL_WAIT	NUMBER
AVERAGE_WAIT	NUMBER

Configuration

The following views provide information about the current configuration of the Oracle environment:

V$COMPATIBILITY

Lists features in use by the current instance that would preclude reverting to a previous release of the Oracle software.

TYPE_ID	VARCHAR2(8)
RELEASE	VARCHAR2(60)
DESCRIPTION	VARCHAR2(64)

NOTE

Because the rows returned by the V$COMPATIBILITY view are instance-based, some of them may not be available if the database has been shut down normally and has not yet been opened.

V$COMPATSEG

Lists permanent features in the database that would preclude reverting to a previous release of the Oracle software.

TYPE_ID	VARCHAR2(8)
RELEASE	VARCHAR2(60)
UPDATED	VARCHAR2(60)

V$EVENT_NAME

Contains descriptive information about all possible wait events.

EVENT#	NUMBER
NAME	VARCHAR2(64)
PARAMETER1	VARCHAR2(64)
PARAMETER2	VARCHAR2(64)
PARAMETER3	VARCHAR2(64)

V$LICENSE

Contains a single row specifying the maximum numbers of concurrent and named users allowed, as well as the high-water marks.

SESSIONS_MAX	NUMBER
SESSIONS_WARNING	NUMBER
SESSIONS_CURRENT	NUMBER
SESSIONS_HIGHWATER	NUMBER
USERS_MAX	NUMBER

V$MLS_PARAMETERS

Lists the initialization parameters and their current values for Trusted Oracle. Available after database is opened.

NUM	NUMBER
NAME	VARCHAR2(64)
TYPE	NUMBER
VALUE	VARCHAR2(512)
ISDEFAULT	VARCHAR2(9)
ISSES_MODIFIABLE	VARCHAR2(5)
ISSYS_MODIFIABLE	VARCHAR2(9)
ISMODIFIED	VARCHAR2(10)

ISADJUSTED	VARCHAR2(5)
DESCRIPTION	VARCHAR2(64)
UPDATE_COMMENT	VARCHAR2(255)

NOTE

The format of the V$MLS_PARAMETERS view is the same as that of V$PARAMETER.

V$NLS_PARAMETERS

Contains the current values for each of the National Language Support (NLS) parameters.

| PARAMETER | VARCHAR2(64) |
| VALUE | VARCHAR2(64) |

V$NLS_VALID_VALUES

Lists the valid values that each of the NLS parameters can take.

| PARAMETER | VARCHAR2(64) |
| VALUE | VARCHAR2(64) |

V$OPTION

Lists the Oracle options that have been installed with the Oracle software.

| PARAMETER | VARCHAR2(64) |
| VALUE | VARCHAR2(64) |

V$PARAMETER

Lists all initialization parameters and their current settings.

NUM	NUMBER
NAME	VARCHAR2(64)
TYPE	NUMBER
VALUE	VARCHAR2(512)
ISDEFAULT	VARCHAR2(9)
ISSES_MODIFIABLE	VARCHAR2(5)
ISSYS_MODIFIABLE	VARCHAR2(9)
ISMODIFIED	VARCHAR2(10)
ISADJUSTED	VARCHAR2(5)
DESCRIPTION	VARCHAR2(64)
UPDATE_COMMENT	VARCHAR2(255)

V$RMAN_CONFIGURATION

Lists the persistent configuration parameters for the Recovery Manager (RMAN), the standard Oracle backup and recovery utility. New with Oracle9*i*.

CONF#	NUMBER
NAME	VARCHAR2(65)
VALUE	VARCHAR2(1025)

V$SPPARAMETER

Lists the contents of the *SPFILE* initialization file. New with Oracle9*i*.

SID	VARCHAR2(80)
NAME	VARCHAR2(80)
VALUE	VARCHAR2(255)
ISSPECIFIED	VARCHAR2(6)
ORDINAL	NUMBER
UPDATE_COMMENT	VARCHAR2(255)

V$STATNAME

Lists the name for each statistic stored in V$MYSTAT, V$SYSSTAT, and V$SESSTAT.

STATISTIC#	NUMBER
NAME	VARCHAR2(64)
CLASS	NUMBER

V$SYSTEM_PARAMETER

Lists all initialization parameters and their current settings.

NUM	NUMBER
NAME	VARCHAR2(64)
TYPE	NUMBER
VALUE	VARCHAR2(512)
ISDEFAULT	VARCHAR2(9)
ISSES_MODIFIABLE	VARCHAR2(5)
ISSYS_MODIFIABLE	VARCHAR2(9)
ISMODIFIED	VARCHAR2(8)
ISADJUSTED	VARCHAR2(5)

| DESCRIPTION | VARCHAR2(64) |
| UPDATE_COMMENT | VARCHAR2(255) |

NOTE

The V$SYSTEM_PARAMETER view also shows whether the current value is specified in the initialization file or is the default value. In addition, it indicates whether the parameter may be modified with an ALTER SYSTEM or ALTER SESSION command. The following query lists parameters that have been specified, along with their values:

```
SELECT name,value
FROM v$system_parameter
WHERE isdefault = 'FALSE';
```

V$TIMEZONE_NAMES

Lists the names and accepted abbreviations for valid time zones for the Oracle database. New with Oracle9*i*.

| TZNAME | VARCHAR2(64) |
| TZABBREV | VARCHAR2(64) |

V$VERSION

Lists current version numbers of the library components of the Oracle kernel.

| BANNER | VARCHAR2(64) |

Data dictionary cache

The following views provide information about how the Oracle kernel is managing the data dictionary and library caches:

V$DB_OBJECT_CACHE

Lists tables, indexes, clusters, synonyms, PL/SQL procedures, packages, and triggers that are in the library cache.

OWNER	VARCHAR2(64)
NAME	VARCHAR2(1000)
DB_LINK	VARCHAR2(64)
NAMESPACE	VARCHAR2(28)
TYPE	VARCHAR2(28)
SHARABLE_MEM	NUMBER
LOADS	NUMBER
EXECUTIONS	NUMBER
LOCKS	NUMBER

PINS	NUMBER
KEPT	VARCHAR2(3)
CHILD_LATCH	NUMBER

V$LIBRARYCACHE

Contains statistics about library cache performance.

NAMESPACE	VARCHAR2(15)
GETS	NUMBER
GETHITS	NUMBER
GETHITRATIO	NUMBER
PINS	NUMBER
PINHITS	NUMBER
PINHITRATIO	NUMBER
RELOADS	NUMBER
INVALIDATIONS	NUMBER
DLM_LOCK_REQUESTS	NUMBER
DLM_PIN_REQUESTS	NUMBER
DLM_PIN_RELEASES	NUMBER
DLM_INVALIDATION_REQUESTS	NUMBER
DLM_INVALIDATIONS	NUMBER

V$ROWCACHE

Contains statistics about data dictionary cache performance.

CACHE#	NUMBER
TYPE	VARCHAR2(11)
SUBORDINATE#	NUMBER
PARAMETER	VARCHAR2(32)
COUNT	NUMBER
USAGE	NUMBER
FIXED	NUMBER
GETS	NUMBER
GETMISSES	NUMBER
SCANS	NUMBER
SCANMISSES	NUMBER
SCANCOMPLETES	NUMBER
MODIFICATIONS	NUMBER
FLUSHES	NUMBER
DLM_REQUESTS	NUMBER
DLM_CONFLICTS	NUMBER
DLM_RELEASES	NUMBER

V$SUBCACHE

Lists each subordinate cache in the library cache.

OWNER_NAME	VARCHAR2(64)
NAME	VARCHAR2(1000)
TYPE	NUMBER
HEAP_NUM	NUMBER
CACHE_ID	NUMBER

CACHE_CNT	NUMBER
HEAP_SZ	NUMBER
HEAP_ALOC	NUMBER
HEAP_USED	NUMBER

Database

The following views provide information about the physical database:

V$CONTROLFILE

Provides the names of all control files.

| STATUS | VARCHAR2(7) |
| NAME | VARCHAR2(513) |

V$CONTROLFILE_RECORD_SECTION

Provides information about the amount of information stored in each section of the control file. Available after database is mounted.

TYPE	VARCHAR2(20)
RECORD_SIZE	NUMBER
RECORDS_TOTAL	NUMBER
RECORDS_USED	NUMBER
FIRST_INDEX	NUMBER
LAST_INDEX	NUMBER
LAST_RECID	NUMBER

V$DATABASE

Provides information about the database that is stored in the control file. Available after database is mounted.

DBID	NUMBER
NAME	VARCHAR2(9)
CREATED	DATE
RESETLOGS_CHANGE#	NUMBER
RESETLOGS_TIME	DATE
PRIOR_RESETLOGS_CHANGE#	NUMBER
PRIOR_RESETLOGS_TIME	DATE
LOG_MODE	VARCHAR2(12)
CHECKPOINT_CHANGE#	NUMBER
ARCHIVE_CHANGE#	NUMBER
CONTROLFILE_TYPE	VARCHAR2(7)
CONTROLFILE_CREATED	DATE
CONTROLFILE_SEQUENCE#	NUMBER
CONTROLFILE_CHANGE#	NUMBER
CONTROLFILE_TIME	DATE
OPEN_RESETLOGS	VARCHAR2(11)
VERSION_TIME	DATE

OPEN_MODE	VARCHAR2(10)
PROTECTION_MODE	VARCHAR2(20)
PROTECTION_LEVEL	VARCHAR2(20)
REMOTE_ARCHIVE	VARCHAR2(8)
ACTIVATION#	NUMBER
DATABASE_ROLE	VARCHAR2(16)
ARCHIVELOG_CHANGE#	NUMBER
SWITCHOVER_STATUS	VARCHAR2(18)
DATAGUARD_BROKER	VARCHAR2(8)
GUARD_STATUS	VARCHAR2(7)
SUPPLEMENTAL_LOG_DATA_MIN	VARCHAR2(3)
SUPPLEMENTAL_LOG_DATA_PK	VARCHAR2(3)
SUPPLEMENTAL_LOG_DATA_UI	VARCHAR2(3)
FORCE_LOGGING	VARCHAR2(3)

V$DATAFILE

Contains information about each datafile, based on information from the control file. Available after database is mounted.

FILE#	NUMBER
CREATION_CHANGE#	NUMBER
CREATION_TIME	DATE
TS#	NUMBER
RFILE#	NUMBER
STATUS	VARCHAR2(7)
ENABLED	VARCHAR2(10)
CHECKPOINT_CHANGE#	NUMBER
CHECKPOINT_TIME	DATE
UNRECOVERABLE_CHANGE#	NUMBER
UNRECOVERABLE_TIME	DATE
LAST_CHANGE#	NUMBER
LAST_TIME	DATE
OFFLINE_CHANGE#	NUMBER
ONLINE_CHANGE#	NUMBER
ONLINE_TIME	DATE
BYTES	NUMBER
BLOCKS	NUMBER
CREATE_BYTES	NUMBER
BLOCK_SIZE	NUMBER
NAME	VARCHAR2(513)
PLUGGED_IN	NUMBER
BLOCK1_OFFSET	NUMBER
AUX_NAME	VARCHAR2(513)

V$DATAFILE_HEADER

Contains information about each datafile, based on information in the datafile header. Available after database is mounted.

FILE#	NUMBER
STATUS	VARCHAR2(7)
ERROR	VARCHAR2(18)
FORMAT	NUMBER
RECOVER	VARCHAR2(3)
FUZZY	VARCHAR2(3)
CREATION_CHANGE#	NUMBER
CREATION_TIME	DATE
TABLESPACE_NAME	VARCHAR2(30)
TS#	NUMBER
RFILE#	NUMBER
RESETLOGS_CHANGE#	NUMBER
RESETLOGS_TIME	DATE
CHECKPOINT_CHANGE#	NUMBER
CHECKPOINT_TIME	DATE
CHECKPOINT_COUNT	NUMBER
BYTES	NUMBER
BLOCKS	NUMBER
NAME	VARCHAR2(513)

V$DBFILE

Contains the name for each datafile. Available after database is mounted.

FILE#	NUMBER
NAME	VARCHAR2(513)

NOTE

The V$DBFILE view is maintained for backward compatibility, but Oracle recommends that you now use V$DATAFILE instead.

V$FILESTAT

Provides information about the I/O activity for each file used in the database. Available after database is mounted. New with Oracle9*i*.

FILE#	NUMBER
PHYRDS	NUMBER
PHYWRTS	NUMBER
PHYBLKRD	NUMBER
PHYBLKWRT	NUMBER
SINGLEBLKRDS	NUMBER
READTIM	NUMBER
WRITETIM	NUMBER
SINGLEBLKRDTIM	NUMBER
AVGIOTIM	NUMBER

LSTIOTIM	NUMBER
MINIOTIM	NUMBER
MAXIORTM	NUMBER
MAXIOWTM	NUMBER

V$OFFLINE_RANGE

Provides information about the offline status of datafiles, based on information provided in the control file. Available after database is mounted.

RECID	NUMBER
STAMP	NUMBER
FILE#	NUMBER
OFFLINE_CHANGE#	NUMBER
ONLINE_CHANGE#	NUMBER
ONLINE_TIME	DATE

V$TABLESPACE

Provides information about tablespaces, based on information in the control file. Available after database is mounted.

TS#	NUMBER
NAME	VARCHAR2(30)
INCLUDED_IN_DATABASE_BACKUP	VARCHAR2(3)

V$TYPE_SIZE

Specifies the size in bytes for the various components of an Oracle data or index block.

COMPONENT	VARCHAR2(8)
TYPE	VARCHAR2(8)
DESCRIPTION	VARCHAR2(32)
TYPE_SIZE	NUMBER

V$UNDOSTAT

Lists a variety of information about the use of undo space by the database. New with Oracle9i.

BEGIN_TIME	DATE
END_TIME	DATE
UNDOTSN	NUMBER
UNDOBLKS	NUMBER
TXNCOUNT	NUMBER
MAXQUERYLEN	NUMBER
MAXCONCURRENCY	NUMBER
UNXPSTEALCNT	NUMBER
UNXPBLKRELCNT	NUMBER
UNXPBLKREUCNT	NUMBER
EXPSTEALCNT	NUMBER
EXPBLKRELCNT	NUMBER
EXPBLKREUCNT	NUMBER

SSOLDERRCNT	NUMBER
NOSPACEERRCNT	NUMBER

NOTE

You can use this information to estimate the amount of undo space needed by the database. It is also used by the database to tune the use of undo space.

Instance

The following views provide information related to the status of the instance:

V$BGPROCESS

Provides information about each of the background processes.

PADDR	RAW(4)
NAME	VARCHAR2(5)
DESCRIPTION	VARCHAR2(64)
ERROR	NUMBER

V$INSTANCE

Provides status information about the current instance.

INSTANCE_NUMBER	NUMBER
INSTANCE_NAME	VARCHAR2(16)
HOST_NAME	VARCHAR2(64)
VERSION	VARCHAR2(17)
STARTUP_TIME	DATE
STATUS	VARCHAR2(12)
PARALLEL	VARCHAR2(3)
THREAD#	NUMBER
ARCHIVER	VARCHAR2(7)
LOG_SWITCH_WAIT	VARCHAR2(11)
LOGINS	VARCHAR2(10)
SHUTDOWN_PENDING	VARCHAR2(3)
DATABASE_STATUS	VARCHAR2(17)
INSTANCE_ROLE	VARCHAR2(18)
ACTIVE_STATE	VARCHAR2(9)

Locks and latches

The following views provide information about the status of locks and latches within the instance:

V$ACCESS

Lists all locked objects in the database and the sessions accessing these objects.

SID	NUMBER
OWNER	VARCHAR2(64)
OBJECT	VARCHAR2(1000)
TYPE	VARCHAR2(24)

V$BUFFER_POOL

Provides information about the available buffer pools.

ID	NUMBER
NAME	VARCHAR2(20)
BLOCK_SIZE	NUMBER
RESIZE_STATE	VARCHAR2(10)
CURRENT_SIZE	NUMBER
BUFFERS	NUMBER
TARGET_SIZE	NUMBER
TARGET_BUFFERS	NUMBER
PREV_SIZE	NUMBER
PREV_BUFFERS	NUMBER
LO_BNUM	NUMBER
HI_BNUM	NUMBER
LO_SETID	NUMBER
HI_SETID	NUMBER
SET_COUNT	NUMBER

NOTE

The number of buffer pools is related to the initialization parameter DB_BLOCK_LRU_LATCHES. You can obtain the value of this parameter from V$PARAMETER or V$_SYSTEM_PARAMETER.

V$ENQUEUE_LOCK

Lists all locks owned by enqueue state objects.

ADDR	RAW(4)
KADDR	RAW(4)
SID	NUMBER
TYPE	VARCHAR2(2)
ID1	NUMBER
ID2	NUMBER
LMODE	NUMBER
REQUEST	NUMBER
CTIME	NUMBER
BLOCK	NUMBER

V$LATCH

Provides statistics for all latches. Available after database is opened.

ADDR	RAW(4)
LATCH#	NUMBER
LEVEL#	NUMBER
NAME	VARCHAR2(64)
GETS	NUMBER
MISSES	NUMBER
SLEEPS	NUMBER
IMMEDIATE_GETS	NUMBER
IMMEDIATE_MISSES	NUMBER
WAITERS_WOKEN	NUMBER
WAITS_HOLDING_LATCH	NUMBER
SPIN_GETS	NUMBER
SLEEP1	NUMBER
SLEEP2	NUMBER
SLEEP3	NUMBER
SLEEP4	NUMBER
SLEEP5	NUMBER
SLEEP6	NUMBER
SLEEP7	NUMBER
SLEEP8	NUMBER
SLEEP9	NUMBER
SLEEP10	NUMBER
SLEEP11	NUMBER
WAIT_TIME	NUMBER

NOTE

If the latch is a parent latch, then the V$LATCH view provides a summation of the statistics for each of its children latches.

V$LATCH_CHILDREN

Provides statistics for all children latches.

ADDR	RAW(4)
LATCH#	NUMBER
CHILD#	NUMBER
LEVEL#	NUMBER
NAME	VARCHAR2(64)
GETS	NUMBER
MISSES	NUMBER
SLEEPS	NUMBER
IMMEDIATE_GETS	NUMBER
IMMEDIATE_MISSES	NUMBER

WAITERS_WOKEN	NUMBER
WAITS_HOLDING_LATCH	NUMBER
SPIN_GETS	NUMBER
SLEEP1	NUMBER
SLEEP2	NUMBER
SLEEP3	NUMBER
SLEEP4	NUMBER
SLEEP5	NUMBER
SLEEP6	NUMBER
SLEEP7	NUMBER
SLEEP8	NUMBER
SLEEP9	NUMBER
SLEEP10	NUMBER
SLEEP11	NUMBER
WAIT_TIME	NUMBER

V$LATCH_MISSES

Provides statistics about all failures to acquire a latch.

PARENT_NAME	VARCHAR2(50)
WHERE	VARCHAR2(64)
NWFAIL_COUNT	NUMBER
SLEEP_COUNT	NUMBER
WTR_SLP_COUNT	NUMBER
LONGHOLD_COUNT	NUMBER

V$LATCH_PARENT

Provides statistics for all parent latches.

ADDR	RAW(4)
LATCH#	NUMBER
LEVEL#	NUMBER
NAME	VARCHAR2(64)
GETS	NUMBER
MISSES	NUMBER
SLEEPS	NUMBER
IMMEDIATE_GETS	NUMBER
IMMEDIATE_MISSES	NUMBER
WAITERS_WOKEN	NUMBER
WAITS_HOLDING_LATCH	NUMBER
SPIN_GETS	NUMBER
SLEEP1	NUMBER
SLEEP2	NUMBER
SLEEP3	NUMBER
SLEEP4	NUMBER
SLEEP5	NUMBER
SLEEP6	NUMBER
SLEEP7	NUMBER
SLEEP8	NUMBER
SLEEP9	NUMBER

SLEEP10	NUMBER
SLEEP11	NUMBER
WAIT_TIME	NUMBER

V$LATCHHOLDER

Provides information about current latch holders.

PID	NUMBER
SID	NUMBER
LADDR	RAW(4)
NAME	VARCHAR2(64)

V$LATCHNAME

Provides a decoded latch name for every latch listed in V$LATCH. Available after database is mounted.

| LATCH# | NUMBER |
| NAME | VARCHAR2(64) |

V$LOCK

Lists all locks held and all outstanding requests for locks or latches.

ADDR	RAW(4)
KADDR	RAW(4)
SID	NUMBER
TYPE	VARCHAR2(2)
ID1	NUMBER
ID2	NUMBER
LMODE	NUMBER
REQUEST	NUMBER
CTIME	NUMBER
BLOCK	NUMBER

V$LOCKED_OBJECT

Lists all objects locked by transactions within the system.

XIDUSN	NUMBER
XIDSLOT	NUMBER
XIDSQN	NUMBER
OBJECT_ID	NUMBER
SESSION_ID	NUMBER
ORACLE_USERNAME	VARCHAR2(30)
OS_USER_NAME	VARCHAR2(30)
PROCESS	VARCHAR2(12)
LOCKED_MODE	NUMBER

V$RESOURCE

Contains the names, types, and addresses of all resources in the system.

ADDR	RAW(4)
TYPE	VARCHAR2(2)
ID1	NUMBER
ID2	NUMBER

Multi-Threaded Server/Shared Servers

The following views provide information on how the Multi-Threaded Server (MTS) or Shared Server (with Oracle9i) systems are configured and performing:

V$CIRCUIT

Contains information about the virtual circuits used to connect users to the instance.

CIRCUIT	RAW(4)
DISPATCHER	RAW(4)
SERVER	RAW(4)
WAITER	RAW(4)
SADDR	RAW(4)
STATUS	VARCHAR2(16)
QUEUE	VARCHAR2(16)
MESSAGE0	NUMBER
MESSAGE1	NUMBER
MESSAGE2	NUMBER
MESSAGE3	NUMBER
MESSAGES	NUMBER
BYTES	NUMBER
BREAKS	NUMBER
PRESENTATION	VARCHAR2(256)
PCIRCUIT	RAW(4)

V$DISPATCHER

Provides information about the various configured dispatcher processes.

NAME	VARCHAR2(4)
NETWORK	VARCHAR2(128)
PADDR	RAW(4)
STATUS	VARCHAR2(16)
ACCEPT	VARCHAR2(3)
MESSAGES	NUMBER
BYTES	NUMBER
BREAKS	NUMBER
OWNED	NUMBER
CREATED	NUMBER
IDLE	NUMBER
BUSY	NUMBER
LISTENER	NUMBER
CONF_INDX	NUMBER

V$DISPATCHER_RATE

Provides statistics about the dispatcher processes throughput.

NAME	VARCHAR2(4)
PADDR	RAW(4)
CUR_LOOP_RATE	NUMBER
CUR_EVENT_RATE	NUMBER
CUR_EVENTS_PER_LOOP	NUMBER
CUR_MSG_RATE	NUMBER
CUR_SVR_BUF_RATE	NUMBER
CUR_SVR_BYTE_RATE	NUMBER
CUR_SVR_BYTE_PER_BUF	NUMBER
CUR_CLT_BUF_RATE	NUMBER
CUR_CLT_BYTE_RATE	NUMBER
CUR_CLT_BYTE_PER_BUF	NUMBER
CUR_BUF_RATE	NUMBER
CUR_BYTE_RATE	NUMBER
CUR_BYTE_PER_BUF	NUMBER
CUR_IN_CONNECT_RATE	NUMBER
CUR_OUT_CONNECT_RATE	NUMBER
CUR_RECONNECT_RATE	NUMBER
MAX_LOOP_RATE	NUMBER
MAX_EVENT_RATE	NUMBER
MAX_EVENTS_PER_LOOP	NUMBER
MAX_MSG_RATE	NUMBER
MAX_SVR_BUF_RATE	NUMBER
MAX_SVR_BYTE_RATE	NUMBER
MAX_SVR_BYTE_PER_BUF	NUMBER
MAX_CLT_BUF_RATE	NUMBER
MAX_CLT_BYTE_RATE	NUMBER
MAX_CLT_BYTE_PER_BUF	NUMBER
MAX_BUF_RATE	NUMBER
MAX_BYTE_RATE	NUMBER
MAX_BYTE_PER_BUF	NUMBER
MAX_IN_CONNECT_RATE	NUMBER
MAX_OUT_CONNECT_RATE	NUMBER
MAX_RECONNECT_RATE	NUMBER
AVG_LOOP_RATE	NUMBER
AVG_EVENT_RATE	NUMBER
AVG_EVENTS_PER_LOOP	NUMBER
AVG_MSG_RATE	NUMBER
AVG_SVR_BUF_RATE	NUMBER
AVG_SVR_BYTE_RATE	NUMBER
AVG_SVR_BYTE_PER_BUF	NUMBER
AVG_CLT_BUF_RATE	NUMBER
AVG_CLT_BYTE_RATE	NUMBER
AVG_CLT_BYTE_PER_BUF	NUMBER
AVG_BUF_RATE	NUMBER
AVG_BYTE_RATE	NUMBER

AVG_BYTE_PER_BUF	NUMBER
AVG_IN_CONNECT_RATE	NUMBER
AVG_OUT_CONNECT_RATE	NUMBER
AVG_RECONNECT_RATE	NUMBER
TTL_LOOPS	NUMBER
TTL_MSG	NUMBER
TTL_SVR_BUF	NUMBER
TTL_CLT_BUF	NUMBER
TTL_BUF	NUMBER
TTL_IN_CONNECT	NUMBER
TTL_OUT_CONNECT	NUMBER
TTL_RECONNECT	NUMBER
SCALE_LOOPS	NUMBER
SCALE_MSG	NUMBER
SCALE_SVR_BUF	NUMBER
SCALE_CLT_BUF	NUMBER
SCALE_BUF	NUMBER
SCALE_IN_CONNECT	NUMBER
SCALE_OUT_CONNECT	NUMBER

V$MTS

Provides information about the overall activity of the Multi-Threaded Server/Shared Server.

MAXIMUM_CONNECTIONS	NUMBER
MAXIMUM_SESSIONS	NUMBER
SERVERS_STARTED	NUMBER
SERVERS_TERMINATED	NUMBER
SERVERS_HIGHWATER	NUMBER

V$QUEUE

Provides statistics about the multi-threaded message queue.

PADDR	RAW(4)
TYPE	VARCHAR2(10)
QUEUED	NUMBER
WAIT	NUMBER
TOTALQ	NUMBER

V$REQDIST

Provides a 12-bucket histogram of the distribution of request service times.

BUCKET	NUMBER
COUNT	NUMBER

V$SHARED_SERVER

Shows the status of the each of the shared servers.

NAME	VARCHAR2(4)
PADDR	RAW(4)
STATUS	VARCHAR2(16)
MESSAGES	NUMBER
BYTES	NUMBER
BREAKS	NUMBER
CIRCUIT	RAW(4)
IDLE	NUMBER
BUSY	NUMBER
REQUESTS	NUMBER

Oracle Parallel Server/Real Application Clusters

The following views are specific to an Oracle Parallel Server/ Real Application Clusters environment:

V$ACTIVE_INSTANCES

Lists all current instances that have the database mounted.

INST_NUMBER	NUMBER
INST_NAME	VARCHAR2(60)

V$BH

Provides the status and pings of every data buffer in the System Global Area (SGA). Available after database is opened.

FILE#	NUMBER
BLOCK#	NUMBER
CLASS#	NUMBER
STATUS	VARCHAR2(5)
XNC	NUMBER
FORCED_READS	NUMBER
FORCED_WRITES	NUMBER
LOCK_ELEMENT_ADDR	RAW(4)
LOCK_ELEMENT_NAME	NUMBER
LOCK_ELEMENT_CLASS	NUMBER
DIRTY	VARCHAR2(1)
TEMP	VARCHAR2(1)

PING	VARCHAR2(1)
STALE	VARCHAR2(1)
DIRECT	VARCHAR2(1)
NEW	CHAR(1)
OBJD	NUMBER
TS#	NUMBER

V$CACHE

Provides information about the block header of every object the current instance has in its SGA. Available after database is opened.

FILE#	NUMBER
BLOCK#	NUMBER
CLASS#	NUMBER
STATUS	VARCHAR2(1)
XNC	NUMBER
FORCED_READS	NUMBER
FORCED_WRITES	NUMBER
NAME	VARCHAR2(30)
PARTITION_NAME	VARCHAR2(30)
KIND	VARCHAR2(12)
OWNER	NUMBER
LOCK_ELEMENT_ADDR	RAW(4)
LOCK_ELEMENT_NAME	NUMBER

V$CACHE_LOCK

Provides the lock status of every data block the current instance has in its SGA. Available after database is opened.

FILE#	NUMBER
BLOCK#	NUMBER
STATUS	VARCHAR2(4)
XNC	NUMBER
NAME	VARCHAR2(30)
KIND	VARCHAR2(12)
OWNER#	NUMBER
LOCK_ELEMENT_ADDR	RAW(4)
FORCED_READS	NUMBER
FORCED_WRITES	NUMBER
INDX	NUMBER
CLASS	NUMBER

V$CLASS_PING

Shows statistics on the number of pings per data block class.

CLASS	VARCHAR2(18)
X_2_NULL	NUMBER
X_2_NULL_FORCED_WRITE	NUMBER
X_2_NULL_FORCED_STALE	NUMBER

X_2_S	NUMBER
X_2_S_FORCED_WRITE	NUMBER
X_2_SSX	NUMBER
X_2_SSX_FORCED_WRITE	NUMBER
S_2_NULL	NUMBER
S_2_NULL_FORCED_STALE	NUMBER
SS_2_NULL	NUMBER
SS_2_RLS	NUMBER
OP_2_SS	NUMBER
NULL_2_X	NUMBER
S_2_X	NUMBER
SSX_2_X	NUMBER
NULL_2_S	NUMBER
NULL_2_SS	NUMBER

V$ENQUEUE_STAT

Lists statistics about each of the different types of enqueue requests for a particular database instance. An enqueue is used to prevent multiple users or processes from writing to the same data block at the same time. New with Oracle9i.

INST_ID	NUMBER
EQ_TYPE	VARCHAR2(2)
TOTAL_REQ#	NUMBER
TOTAL_WAIT#	NUMBER
SUCC_REQ#	NUMBER
FAILED_REQ#	NUMBER
CUM_WAIT_TIME	NUMBER

V$FALSE_PING

Lists buffers that are getting excessive pings, because they are covered under a different lock. Available after database is opened.

FILE#	NUMBER
BLOCK#	NUMBER
STATUS	VARCHAR2(1)
XNC	NUMBER
FORCED_READS	NUMBER
FORCED_WRITES	NUMBER
NAME	VARCHAR2(30)
PARTITION_NAME	VARCHAR2(30)
KIND	VARCHAR2(12)
OWNER	NUMBER
LOCK_ELEMENT_ADDR	RAW(4)
LOCK_ELEMENT_NAME	NUMBER
LOCK_ELEMENT_CLASS	NUMBER

V$FILE_CACHE_TRANSFER

Shows the number of block pings per datafile. Available after database is mounted.

FILE_NUMBER	NUMBER
X_2_NULL	NUMBER
X_2_NULL_FORCED_WRITE	NUMBER
X_2_NULL_FORCED_STALE	NUMBER
X_2_S	NUMBER
X_2_S_FORCED_WRITE	NUMBER
S_2_NULL	NUMBER
S_2_NULL_FORCED_STALE	NUMBER
RBR	NUMBER
RBR_FORCED_WRITE	NUMBER
RBR_FORCED_STALE	NUMBER
NULL_2_X	NUMBER
S_2_X	NUMBER
NULL_2_S	NUMBER
CR_TRANSFERS	NUMBER
CUR_TRANSFERS	NUMBER

V$GCSHVMASTER_INFO

Tracks the mastering of Global Cache Service resources, for those in files that are mapped to a specific instance. New with Oracle9*i*.

HV_ID	NUMBER
CURRENT_MASTER	NUMBER
PREVIOUS_MASTER	NUMBER
REMASTER_CNT	NUMBER

V$GCSPFMASTER_INFO

Tracks the mastering of Global Cache Service resources in files that are mapped to a specific instance. New with Oracle9*i*.

FILE_ID	NUMBER
CURRENT_MASTER	NUMBER
PREVIOUS_MASTER	NUMBER
REMASTER_CNT	NUMBER

V$GES_CONVERT_LOCAL

Shows elapsed times for local DLM lock conversions.

INST_ID	NUMBER
CONVERT_TYPE	VARCHAR2(16)
AVERAGE_CONVERT_TIME	NUMBER
CONVERT_COUNT	NUMBER

NOTE

Prior to Oracle9*i* the V$GES_CONVERT_LOCAL view was called V$DLM_CONVERT_LOCAL.

V$GES_CONVERT_REMOTE

Shows elapsed times for remote DLM lock conversions.

INST_ID	NUMBER
CONVERT_TYPE	VARCHAR2(16)
AVERAGE_CONVERT_TIME	NUMBER
CONVERT_COUNT	NUMBER

NOTE

Prior to Oracle9*i* the V$GES_CONVERT_REMOTE view was called V$DLM_CONVERT_REMOTE.

V$GES_LATCH

Shows the total count and number of immediate gets of DLM latches acquired by latch type Available after database is opened.

ADDR	RAW(4)
LATCH#	NUMBER
LEVEL#	NUMBER
NAME	VARCHAR2(64)
GETS	NUMBER
MISSES	NUMBER
SLEEPS	NUMBER
IMMEDIATE_GETS	NUMBER
IMMEDIATE_MISSES	NUMBER
WAITERS_WOKEN	NUMBER
WAITS_HOLDING_LATCH	NUMBER

SPIN_GETS	NUMBER
SLEEP1	NUMBER
SLEEP2	NUMBER
SLEEP3	NUMBER
SLEEP4	NUMBER
SLEEP5	NUMBER
SLEEP6	NUMBER
SLEEP7	NUMBER
SLEEP8	NUMBER
SLEEP9	NUMBER
SLEEP10	NUMBER
SLEEP11	NUMBER
WAIT_TIME	NUMBER

NOTE

Prior to Oracle9*i* the V$GES_LATCH view was called V$DLM_LATCH.

V$GES_LOCKS

Shows all DLM locks and lock requests that are blocked or are blocking other lock requests.

LOCKP	RAW(4)
GRANT_LEVEL	VARCHAR2(9)
REQUEST_LEVEL	VARCHAR2(9)
RESOURCE_NAME1	VARCHAR2(30)
RESOURCE_NAME2	VARCHAR2(30)
PID	NUMBER
TRANSACTION_ID0	NUMBER
TRANSACTION_ID1	NUMBER
GROUP_ID	NUMBER
OPEN_OPT_DEADLOCK	NUMBER
OPEN_OPT_PERSISTENT	NUMBER
OPEN_OPT_PROCESS_OWNED	NUMBER
OPEN_OPT_NO_XID	NUMBER
CONVERT_OPT_GETVALUE	NUMBER
CONVERT_OPT_PUTVALUE	NUMBER
CONVERT_OPT_NOVALUE	NUMBER
CONVERT_OPT_DUBVALUE	NUMBER
CONVERT_OPT_NOQUEUE	NUMBER
CONVERT_OPT_EXPRESS	NUMBER
CONVERT_OPT_NODEADLOCKWAIT	NUMBER
CONVERT_OPT_NODEADLOCKBLOCK	NUMBER
WHICH_QUEUE	NUMBER
LOCKSTATE	VARCHAR2(64)
AST_EVENT0	NUMBER

OWNER_NODE	NUMBER
BLOCKED	NUMBER
BLOCKER	NUMBER

NOTE

Prior to Oracle9*i* the V$GES_LOCKS view was called V$DLM_LOCKS.

V$GES_MISC

Provides statistics on various DLM parameters.

STATISTIC#	NUMBER
NAME	VARCHAR2(38)
VALUE	NUMBER

NOTE

Prior to Oracle9*i* the V$GES_MISC view was called V$DLM_MISC.

V$HVMASTER_INFO

Tracks the mastering of Global Enqueue Service resources. New with Oracle9*i*.

HV_ID	NUMBER
CURRENT_MASTER	NUMBER
PREVIOUS_MASTER	NUMBER
REMASTER_CNT	NUMBER

V$LOCK_ACTIVITY

Provides an overall view of DLM locks within the current instance.

FROM_VAL	VARCHAR2(4)
TO_VAL	VARCHAR2(4)
ACTION_VAL	VARCHAR2(50)
COUNTER	NUMBER

V$LOCK_ELEMENT

Provides information about each PCM lock in the data buffers.

LOCK_ELEMENT_ADDR	RAW(4)
INDX	NUMBER
CLASS	NUMBER
LOCK_ELEMENT_NAME	NUMBER
MODE_HELD	NUMBER

BLOCK_COUNT	NUMBER
RELEASING	NUMBER
ACQUIRING	NUMBER
INVALID	NUMBER
FLAGS	NUMBER

V$LOCKS_WITH_COLLISIONS

Shows locks with a high numbers of false pings.

| LOCK_ELEMENT_ADDR | RAW(4) |

V$PING

A subset of V$CACHE; shows only those buffers that have been pinged at least once. Available after database is opened.

FILE#	NUMBER
BLOCK#	NUMBER
CLASS#	NUMBER
STATUS	VARCHAR2(1)
XNC	NUMBER
FORCED_READS	NUMBER
FORCED_WRITES	NUMBER
NAME	VARCHAR2(30)
PARTITION_NAME	VARCHAR2(30)
KIND	VARCHAR2(12)
OWNER	NUMBER
LOCK_ELEMENT_ADDR	RAW(4)
LOCK_ELEMENT_NAME	NUMBER

NOTE

The V$PING view is identical to the V$CACHE view, but it displays only blocks that have been pinged at least once. This view contains information from the block header of each block in the SGA of the current instance as related to particular database objects.

Parallel Query

The following views provide information in support of Parallel Query operations:

V$EXECUTION

Provides information about each Parallel Query execution.

PID	NUMBER
DEPTH	NUMBER
FUNCTION	VARCHAR2(10)

TYPE	VARCHAR2(7)
NVALS	NUMBER
VAL1	NUMBER
VAL2	NUMBER
SEQH	NUMBER
SEQL	NUMBER

V$PQ_SESSTAT

Provides statistics on Parallel Query activity for the current session.

STATISTIC	VARCHAR2(30)
LAST_QUERY	NUMBER
SESSION_TOTAL	NUMBER

V$PQ_SLAVE

Provides statistics on each of the Parallel Query servers in the system.

SLAVE_NAME	VARCHAR2(4)
STATUS	VARCHAR2(4)
SESSIONS	NUMBER
IDLE_TIME_CUR	NUMBER
BUSY_TIME_CUR	NUMBER
CPU_SECS_CUR	NUMBER
MSGS_SENT_CUR	NUMBER
MSGS_RCVD_CUR	NUMBER
IDLE_TIME_TOTAL	NUMBER
BUSY_TIME_TOTAL	NUMBER
CPU_SECS_TOTAL	NUMBER
MSGS_SENT_TOTAL	NUMBER
MSGS_RCVD_TOTAL	NUMBER

V$PQ_SYSSTAT

Provides a summary of Parallel Query statistics for the entire system.

STATISTIC	VARCHAR2(30)
VALUE	NUMBER

V$PQ_TQSTAT

Provides statistics for each Parallel Query session while it is active.

DFO_NUMBER	NUMBER
TQ_ID	NUMBER
SERVER_TYPE	VARCHAR2(10)
NUM_ROWS	NUMBER
BYTES	NUMBER
OPEN_TIME	NUMBER
AVG_LATENCY	NUMBER

WAITS	NUMBER
TIMEOUTS	NUMBER
PROCESS	VARCHAR2(10)
INSTANCE	NUMBER

Recovery

The following views provide information about the current status of the online and offline redo logs, as well as backup processes controlled by the Recovery Manager (RMAN):

V$ARCHIVE

Lists redo logs that must be archived. Available after database is mounted.

GROUP#	NUMBER
THREAD#	NUMBER
SEQUENCE#	NUMBER
ISCURRENT	VARCHAR2(3)
CURRENT	VARCHAR2(3)
FIRST_CHANGE#	NUMBER

V$ARCHIVE_DEST

Shows the status of all archive log destinations specified for the instance.

DEST_ID	NUMBER
DEST_NAME	VARCHAR2(256)
STATUS	VARCHAR2(9)
BINDING	VARCHAR2(9)
NAME_SPACE	VARCHAR2(7)
TARGET	VARCHAR2(7)
ARCHIVER	VARCHAR2(10)
SCHEDULE	VARCHAR2(8)
DESTINATION	VARCHAR2(256)
LOG_SEQUENCE	NUMBER
REOPEN_SECS	NUMBER
DELAY_MINS	NUMBER
NET_TIMEOUT	NUMBER
PROCESS	VARCHAR2(10)
REGISTER	VARCHAR2(3)
FAIL_DATE	DATE
FAIL_SEQUENCE	NUMBER
FAIL_BLOCK	NUMBER
FAILURE_COUNT	NUMBER
MAX_FAILURE	NUMBER
ERROR	VARCHAR2(256)
ALTERNATE	VARCHAR2(256)
DEPENDENCY	VARCHAR2(256)

REMOTE_TEMPLATE	VARCHAR2(256)
QUOTA_SIZE	NUMBER
QUOTA_USED	NUMBER
MOUNTID	NUMBER
TRANSMIT_MODE	VARCHAR2(12)
ASYNC_BLOCKS	NUMBER
AFFIRM	VARCHAR2(3)
TYPE	VARCHAR2(7)

V$ARCHIVE_DEST_STATUS

Provides runtime information about archived log redo destinations. New with Oracle9i.

DEST_ID	NUMBER
DEST_NAME	VARCHAR2(256)
STATUS	VARCHAR2(9)
TYPE	VARCHAR2(14)
DATABASE_MODE	VARCHAR2(15)
RECOVERY_MODE	VARCHAR2(7)
PROTECTION_MODE	VARCHAR2(20)
DESTINATION	VARCHAR2(256)
STANDBY_LOGFILE_COUNT	NUMBER
STANDBY_LOGFILE_ACTIVE	NUMBER
ARCHIVED_THREAD#	NUMBER
ARCHIVED_SEQ#	NUMBER
APPLIED_THREAD#	NUMBER
APPLIED_SEQ#	NUMBER
ERROR	VARCHAR2(256)
SRL	VARCHAR2(3)

NOTE

You can use the V$ARCHIVE_DESC_STATUS view to see the progress of archiving multiple redo logs to multiple locations.

V$ARCHIVE_GAP

Provides information about gaps in archived redo logs, which can block database recovery operations. New with Oracle9i.

THREAD#	NUMBER
LOW_SEQUENCE#	NUMBER
HIGH_SEQUENCE#	NUMBER

V$ARCHIVED_LOG

Provides information from the control file for all archive logs, using a time-based view of the log files. Available after database is mounted.

RECID	NUMBER
STAMP	NUMBER
NAME	VARCHAR2(513)
DEST_ID	NUMBER
THREAD#	NUMBER
SEQUENCE#	NUMBER
RESETLOGS_CHANGE#	NUMBER
RESETLOGS_TIME	DATE
FIRST_CHANGE#	NUMBER
FIRST_TIME	DATE
NEXT_CHANGE#	NUMBER
NEXT_TIME	DATE
BLOCKS	NUMBER
BLOCK_SIZE	NUMBER
CREATOR	VARCHAR2(7)
REGISTRAR	VARCHAR2(7)
STANDBY_DEST	VARCHAR2(3)
ARCHIVED	VARCHAR2(3)
APPLIED	VARCHAR2(3)
DELETED	VARCHAR2(3)
STATUS	VARCHAR2(1)
COMPLETION_TIME	DATE
DICTIONARY_BEGIN	VARCHAR2(3)
DICTIONARY_END	VARCHAR2(3)
END_OF_REDO	VARCHAR2(3)
BACKUP_COUNT	NUMBER
ARCHIVAL_THREAD#	NUMBER
ACTIVATION#	NUMBER

V$BACKUP

Shows the backup status of all online datafiles managed by RMAN. Available after database is mounted.

FILE#	NUMBER
STATUS	VARCHAR2(18)
CHANGE#	NUMBER
TIME	DATE

V$BACKUP_CORRUPTION

Details any datafile corruption detected as part of a backup managed by RMAN. Available after database is mounted.

RECID	NUMBER
STAMP	NUMBER
SET_STAMP	NUMBER
SET_COUNT	NUMBER
PIECE#	NUMBER
FILE#	NUMBER
BLOCK#	NUMBER
BLOCKS	NUMBER

CORRUPTION_CHANGE#	NUMBER
MARKED_CORRUPT	VARCHAR2(3)
CORRUPTION_TYPE	VARCHAR2(9)

V$BACKUP_DATAFILE

Shows the location of the backup datafile used by RMAN. Available after database is mounted.

RECID	NUMBER
STAMP	NUMBER
SET_STAMP	NUMBER
SET_COUNT	NUMBER
FILE#	NUMBER
CREATION_CHANGE#	NUMBER
CREATION_TIME	DATE
RESETLOGS_CHANGE#	NUMBER
RESETLOGS_TIME	DATE
INCREMENTAL_LEVEL	NUMBER
INCREMENTAL_CHANGE#	NUMBER
CHECKPOINT_CHANGE#	NUMBER
CHECKPOINT_TIME	DATE
ABSOLUTE_FUZZY_CHANGE#	NUMBER
MARKED_CORRUPT	NUMBER
MEDIA_CORRUPT	NUMBER
LOGICALLY_CORRUPT	NUMBER
DATAFILE_BLOCKS	NUMBER
BLOCKS	NUMBER
BLOCK_SIZE	NUMBER
OLDEST_OFFLINE_RANGE	NUMBER
COMPLETION_TIME	DATE
CONTROLFILE_TYPE	VARCHAR2(1)

V$BACKUP_DEVICE

Provides a list of available backup devices supported by RMAN.

DEVICE_TYPE	VARCHAR2(17)
DEVICE_NAME	VARCHAR2(513)

V$BACKUP_PIECE

Provides information about each backup piece (a subset of an RMAN backup set). Available after database is mounted.

RECID	NUMBER
STAMP	NUMBER
SET_STAMP	NUMBER
SET_COUNT	NUMBER
PIECE#	NUMBER
COPY#	NUMBER
DEVICE_TYPE	VARCHAR2(17)
HANDLE	VARCHAR2(513)

COMMENTS	VARCHAR2(81)
MEDIA	VARCHAR2(65)
MEDIA_POOL	NUMBER
CONCUR	VARCHAR2(3)
TAG	VARCHAR2(32)
STATUS	VARCHAR2(1)
START_TIME	DATE
COMPLETION_TIME	DATE
ELAPSED_SECONDS	NUMBER
DELETED	VARCHAR2(3)

V$BACKUP_REDOLOG

Provides information about archived redo logs that have been backed up by RMAN. Available after database is mounted.

RECID	NUMBER
STAMP	NUMBER
SET_STAMP	NUMBER
SET_COUNT	NUMBER
THREAD#	NUMBER
SEQUENCE#	NUMBER
RESETLOGS_CHANGE#	NUMBER
RESETLOGS_TIME	DATE
FIRST_CHANGE#	NUMBER
FIRST_TIME	DATE
NEXT_CHANGE#	NUMBER
NEXT_TIME	DATE
BLOCKS	NUMBER
BLOCK_SIZE	NUMBER

V$BACKUP_SET

Provides information about all RMAN backup sets. Available after database is mounted.

RECID	NUMBER
STAMP	NUMBER
SET_STAMP	NUMBER
SET_COUNT	NUMBER
BACKUP_TYPE	VARCHAR2(1)
CONTROLFILE_INCLUDED	VARCHAR2(3)
INCREMENTAL_LEVEL	NUMBER
PIECES	NUMBER
START_TIME	DATE
COMPLETION_TIME	DATE
ELAPSED_SECONDS	NUMBER
BLOCK_SIZE	NUMBER
INPUT_FILE_SCAN_ONLY	VARCHAR2(3)
KEEP	VARCHAR2(3)
KEEP_UNTIL	DATE
KEEP_OPTIONS	VARCHAR2(10)

V$COPY_CORRUPTION

Details any datafile corruption detected as part of a datafile copy managed by RMAN. Available after database is mounted.

RECID	NUMBER
STAMP	NUMBER
COPY_RECID	NUMBER
COPY_STAMP	NUMBER
FILE#	NUMBER
BLOCK#	NUMBER
BLOCKS	NUMBER
CORRUPTION_CHANGE#	NUMBER
MARKED_CORRUPT	VARCHAR2(3)
CORRUPTION_TYPE	VARCHAR2(9)

V$DATAFILE_COPY

Provides information about datafile copies from the control file. This information is maintained by RMAN. Available after database is mounted.

RECID	NUMBER
STAMP	NUMBER
NAME	VARCHAR2(513)
TAG	VARCHAR2(32)
FILE#	NUMBER
RFILE#	NUMBER
CREATION_CHANGE#	NUMBER
CREATION_TIME	DATE
RESETLOGS_CHANGE#	NUMBER
RESETLOGS_TIME	DATE
INCREMENTAL_LEVEL	NUMBER
CHECKPOINT_CHANGE#	NUMBER
CHECKPOINT_TIME	DATE
ABSOLUTE_FUZZY_CHANGE#	NUMBER
RECOVERY_FUZZY_CHANGE#	NUMBER
RECOVERY_FUZZY_TIME	DATE
ONLINE_FUZZY	VARCHAR2(3)
BACKUP_FUZZY	VARCHAR2(3)
MARKED_CORRUPT	NUMBER
MEDIA_CORRUPT	NUMBER
LOGICALLY_CORRUPT	NUMBER
BLOCKS	NUMBER
BLOCK_SIZE	NUMBER
OLDEST_OFFLINE_RANGE	NUMBER
DELETED	VARCHAR2(3)
STATUS	VARCHAR2(1)
COMPLETION_TIME	DATE
CONTROLFILE_TYPE	VARCHAR2(1)

KEEP	VARCHAR2(3)
KEEP_UNTIL	DATE
KEEP_OPTIONS	VARCHAR2(10)
SCANNED	VARCHAR2(3)

V$DELETED_OBJECT

Provides information about archived redo logs, datafile pieces, and datafile copies that have been deleted from the control file. Available after database is mounted.

RECID	NUMBER
STAMP	NUMBER
TYPE	VARCHAR2(26)
OBJECT_RECID	NUMBER
OBJECT_STAMP	NUMBER
OBJECT_DATA	NUMBER

V$LOG

Contains information about redo logs from the control file. Available after database is mounted.

GROUP#	NUMBER
THREAD#	NUMBER
SEQUENCE#	NUMBER
BYTES	NUMBER
MEMBERS	NUMBER
ARCHIVED	VARCHAR2(3)
STATUS	VARCHAR2(16)
FIRST_CHANGE#	NUMBER
FIRST_TIME	DATE

V$LOG_HISTORY

Contains information about archived redo logs from the control file. Provides a System Change Number (SCN) view of the archived log files. Available after database is mounted.

RECID	NUMBER
STAMP	NUMBER
THREAD#	NUMBER
SEQUENCE#	NUMBER
FIRST_CHANGE#	NUMBER
FIRST_TIME	DATE
NEXT_CHANGE#	NUMBER

V$LOGFILE

Provides the current status of all redo logs. Available after database is mounted.

| GROUP# | NUMBER |
| STATUS | VARCHAR2(7) |

| TYPE | VARCHAR2(7) |
| MEMBER | VARCHAR2(513) |

V$LOGHIST

Contains redo log history from the control file. Available after database is mounted.

THREAD#	NUMBER
SEQUENCE#	NUMBER
FIRST_CHANGE#	NUMBER
FIRST_TIME	DATE
SWITCH_CHANGE#	NUMBER

NOTE

Oracle Corporation recommends that you now use V$LOG_HISTORY instead.

V$MANAGED_STANDBY

Contains information about various Data Guard processes. New with Oracle9i.

THREAD#	NUMBER
SEQUENCE#	NUMBER
FIRST_CHANGE#	NUMBER
FIRST_TIME	DATE
SWITCH_CHANGE#	NUMBER

NOTE

The V$MANAGED_STANDBY view can also be used to monitor the process of recovery with Data Guard

---

V$RECOVER_FILE

Lists datafiles used in media recovery. Available after database is mounted.

FILE#	NUMBER
ONLINE	VARCHAR2(7)
ONLINE_STATUS	VARCHAR2(7)
ERROR	VARCHAR2(18)
CHANGE#	NUMBER
TIME	DATE

V$RECOVERY_FILE_STATUS

Contains information relevant to the current file recovery process. Available after database is mounted.

FILENUM	NUMBER
FILENAME	VARCHAR2(513)
STATUS	VARCHAR2(13)

NOTE

The V$RECOVERY_FILE_STATUS view is only available to the current process and returns no rows when it is queried by another process.

V$RECOVERY_LOG

Contains derived information from V$LOG_HISTORY that is useful to the RMAN process. Available after database is mounted.

THREAD#	NUMBER
SEQUENCE#	NUMBER
TIME	DATE
ARCHIVE_NAME	VARCHAR2(513)

NOTE

The V$RECOVERY_LOG view is only available to the current process and returns no rows when it is queried by another process.

V$RECOVERY_PROGRESS

Contains a subset of V$SESSION_LONGOPS that provides the current status of recovery operations.

TYPE	VARCHAR2(64)
ITEM	VARCHAR2(32)
SOFAR	NUMBER
TOTAL	NUMBER

V$RECOVERY_STATUS

Maintains current statistics for the recovery process.

RECOVERY_CHECKPOINT	DATE
THREAD	NUMBER
SEQUENCE_NEEDED	NUMBER
SCN_NEEDED	VARCHAR2(16)
TIME_NEEDED	DATE
PREVIOUS_LOG_NAME	VARCHAR2(513)
PREVIOUS_LOG_STATUS	VARCHAR2(13)
REASON	VARCHAR2(13)

V$STANDBY_LOG

Lists information on the redo logs for a standby database. New with Oracle*9i*.

GROUP#	NUMBER
THREAD#	NUMBER
SEQUENCE#	NUMBER
BYTES	NUMBER
USED	NUMBER
ARCHIVED	VARCHAR2(3)
STATUS	VARCHAR2(10)
FIRST_CHANGE#	NUMBER
FIRST_TIME	DATE
LAST_CHANGE#	NUMBER
LAST_TIME	DATE

V$THREAD

Contains information about all current redo log threads from the control file. Available after database is mounted.

THREAD#	NUMBER
STATUS	VARCHAR2(6)
ENABLED	VARCHAR2(8)
GROUPS	NUMBER
INSTANCE	VARCHAR2(16)
OPEN_TIME	DATE
CURRENT_GROUP#	NUMBER
SEQUENCE#	NUMBER
CHECKPOINT_CHANGE#	NUMBER
CHECKPOINT_TIME	DATE
ENABLE_CHANGE#	NUMBER
ENABLE_TIME	DATE
DISABLE_CHANGE#	NUMBER
DISABLE_TIME	DATE

Replication

The following views have been added to Oracle9*i* to help monitor and understand the use of replication in the database:

V$MVREFRESH

Provides information about any materialized views that are currently being refreshed. New with Oracle9i.

SID	NUMBER
SERIAL#	NUMBER
CURRMVOWNER	VARCHAR2(31)
CURRMVNAME	VARCHAR2(31)

V$REPLPROP

Provides information about how parallel propagation is operating as part of the replication process. New with Oracle9i.

SID	NUMBER
SERIAL#	NUMBER
NAME	VARCHAR2(71)
DBLINK	VARCHAR2(128)
STATE	VARCHAR2(12)
XID	VARCHAR2(22)
SEQUENCE	NUMBER

V$REPLQUEUE

Provides information about any deferred replication transactions. New with Oracle9i.

TXNS_ENQUEUED	NUMBER
CALLS_ENQUEUED	NUMBER
TXNS_PURGED	NUMBER
LAST_ENQUEUE_TIME	DATE
LAST_PURGE_TIME	DATE

Resource allocation

The Database Resource Manager (DRM) can be used to set up rules for how to allocate resources between different groups of users. With Oracle9i, there are two dynamic views that allow you to see the available resource allocation methods:

V$ACTIVE_SESS_POOL_MTH

Lists all of the currently available active session pool resource allocation methods. New with Oracle9i.

NAME	VARCHAR2(40)

V$QUEUEING_MTH

Lists all of the currently available queuing resource allocation methods. New with Oracle9i.

NAME	VARCHAR2(40)

Security

The following views provide information about privileges:

V$ENABLEDPRIVS

Lists all system privileges that are enabled for the current session.

PRIV_NUMBER	NUMBER

NOTE

The V$ENABLEDPRIVS view includes those privileges explicitly granted as well as those available through a role.

V$PWFILE_USERS

Lists all users who have been identified in the password file as having SYSDBA or SYSOPER privileges.

USERNAME	VARCHAR2(30)
SYSDBA	VARCHAR2(5)
SYSOPER	VARCHAR2(5)

NOTE

Because the password file is encrypted and not directly readable, this view provides a convenient method for examining the contents.

Session

The following views provide information about the current Oracle session:

V$MYSTAT

Provides information about current session statistics.

SID	NUMBER
STATISTIC#	NUMBER
VALUE	NUMBER

There is a one-to-one correspondence between the rows of this view and the rows of V$STATNAME (shown earlier under "Configuration"), so the statistics can be displayed by name with a query like this one:

```
SELECT name,value
FROM v$mystat a, v$statname b
WHERE a.statistic# = b.statistic#;
```

V$PROCESS

Lists information about each process in the instance.

ADDR	RAW(4)
PID	NUMBER
SPID	VARCHAR2(12)
USERNAME	VARCHAR2(15)
SERIAL#	NUMBER
TERMINAL	VARCHAR2(30)
PROGRAM	VARCHAR2(48)
TRACEID	VARCHAR2(255)
BACKGROUND	VARCHAR2(1)
LATCHWAIT	VARCHAR2(8)
LATCHSPIN	VARCHAR2(8)
PGA_USED_MEM	NUMBER
PGA_ALLOC_MEM	NUMBER
PGA_FREEABLE_MEM	NUMBER
PGA_MAX_MEM	NUMBER

You can join the V$PROCESS view to V$SESSION to gain more information about running processes.

V$SESS_IO

Provides up-to-date I/O information for each session in the database. Available after database is opened.

SID	NUMBER
BLOCK_GETS	NUMBER
CONSISTENT_GETS	NUMBER
PHYSICAL_READS	NUMBER
BLOCK_CHANGES	NUMBER
CONSISTENT_CHANGES	NUMBER

V$SESSION

Lists each session in the instance.

SADDR	RAW(4)
SID	NUMBER
SERIAL#	NUMBER
AUDSID	NUMBER
PADDR	RAW(4)
USER#	NUMBER
USERNAME	VARCHAR2(30)
COMMAND	NUMBER
OWNERID	NUMBER
TADDR	VARCHAR2(8)
LOCKWAIT	VARCHAR2(8)
STATUS	VARCHAR2(8)
SERVER	VARCHAR2(9)
SCHEMA#	NUMBER
SCHEMANAME	VARCHAR2(30)
OSUSER	VARCHAR2(30)
PROCESS	VARCHAR2(12)
MACHINE	VARCHAR2(64)
TERMINAL	VARCHAR2(30)
PROGRAM	VARCHAR2(48)
TYPE	VARCHAR2(10)
SQL_ADDRESS	RAW(4)
SQL_HASH_VALUE	NUMBER
PREV_SQL_ADDR	RAW(4)
PREV_HASH_VALUE	NUMBER
MODULE	VARCHAR2(48)
MODULE_HASH	NUMBER
ACTION	VARCHAR2(32)
ACTION_HASH	NUMBER
CLIENT_INFO	VARCHAR2(64)
FIXED_TABLE_SEQUENCE	NUMBER
ROW_WAIT_OBJ#	NUMBER
ROW_WAIT_FILE#	NUMBER
ROW_WAIT_BLOCK#	NUMBER
ROW_WAIT_ROW#	NUMBER
LOGON_TIME	DATE
LAST_CALL_ET	NUMBER
PDML_ENABLED	VARCHAR2(3)
FAILOVER_TYPE	VARCHAR2(13)
FAILOVER_METHOD	VARCHAR2(10)
FAILED_OVER	VARCHAR2(3)
RESOURCE_CONSUMER_GROUP	VARCHAR2(32)
PDML_STATUS	VARCHAR2(8)
PDDL_STATUS	VARCHAR2(8)
PQ_STATUS	VARCHAR2(8)
CURRENT_QUEUE_DURATION	NUMBER
CLIENT_IDENTIFIER	VARCHAR2(64)

V$SESSION_CONNECT_INFO

Provides information about the network connection of the current session.

SID	NUMBER
AUTHENTICATION_TYPE	VARCHAR2(26)
OSUSER	VARCHAR2(30)
NETWORK_SERVICE_BANNER	VARCHAR2(4000)

V$SESSION_CURSOR_CACHE

Provides information about the current session's cursor usage.

MAXIMUM	NUMBER
COUNT	NUMBER
OPENED_ONCE	NUMBER
OPEN	NUMBER
OPENS	NUMBER
HITS	NUMBER
HIT_RATIO	NUMBER

V$SESSION_EVENT

Provides information about how much time each session spends waiting on each event specified in V$EVENT_NAME.

SID	NUMBER
EVENT	VARCHAR2(64)
TOTAL_WAITS	NUMBER
TOTAL_TIMEOUTS	NUMBER
TIME_WAITED	NUMBER
AVERAGE_WAIT	NUMBER
MAX_WAIT	NUMBER
TIME_WAITED_MICRO	NUMBER

V$SESSION_LONGOPS

Provides information about the status of long-running operations for sessions.

SID	NUMBER
SERIAL#	NUMBER
OPNAME	VARCHAR2(64)
TARGET	VARCHAR2(64)
TARGET_DESC	VARCHAR2(32)
SOFAR	NUMBER
TOTALWORK	NUMBER
UNITS	VARCHAR2(32)
START_TIME	DATE
LAST_UPDATE_TIME	DATE
TIME_REMAINING	NUMBER
ELAPSED_SECONDS	NUMBER
CONTEXT	NUMBER
MESSAGE	VARCHAR2(512)
USERNAME	VARCHAR2(30)

SQL_ADDRESS	RAW(4)
SQL_HASH_VALUE	NUMBER
QCSID	NUMBER

NOTE

The V$SESSION_LONGOPS view provides information on the number of work units already accomplished and the expected amount of work required to complete the operation.

V$SESSION_OBJECT_CACHE

Provides object cache statistics for the current session in the current instance.

PINS	NUMBER
HITS	NUMBER
TRUE_HITS	NUMBER
HIT_RATIO	NUMBER
TRUE_HIT_RATIO	NUMBER
OBJECT_REFRESHES	NUMBER
CACHE_REFRESHES	NUMBER
OBJECT_FLUSHES	NUMBER
CACHE_FLUSHES	NUMBER
CACHE_SHRINKS	NUMBER
CACHED_OBJECTS	NUMBER
PINNED_OBJECTS	NUMBER
CACHE_SIZE	NUMBER
OPTIMAL_SIZE	NUMBER
MAXIMUM_SIZE	NUMBER

V$SESSION_WAIT

Lists the resources on which each active session is waiting and how long each session has been waiting for each resource.

SID	NUMBER
SEQ#	NUMBER
EVENT	VARCHAR2(64)
P1TEXT	VARCHAR2(64)
P1	NUMBER
P1RAW	RAW(4)
P2TEXT	VARCHAR2(64)
P2	NUMBER
P2RAW	RAW(4)
P3TEXT	VARCHAR2(64)
P3	NUMBER
P3RAW	RAW(4)
WAIT_TIME	NUMBER
SECONDS_IN_WAIT	NUMBER
STATE	VARCHAR2(19)

V$SESSTAT

Provides information about each session's session statistics.

SID	NUMBER
STATISTIC#	NUMBER
VALUE	NUMBER

System Global Area

The following views provide information about the System Global Area (SGA):

V$PGASTAT

Provides memory usage statistics that are used by the Oracle memory manager to allocate the maximum amount of memory a particular work area is permitted to have at any one time. New with Oracle9i.

NAME	VARCHAR2(64)
VALUE	NUMBER
UNIT	VARCHAR2(12)

V$SGA

Contains information about the size, in bytes, of each of the various SGA components.

NAME	VARCHAR2(20)
VALUE	NUMBER

V$SGASTAT

Provides more detailed information about SGA utilization than V$SGA.

POOL	VARCHAR2(11)
NAME	VARCHAR2(26)
BYTES	NUMBER

NOTE

The V$SGASTAT view is useful because it shows the breakdown of the SHARED_POOL and LARGE_POOL areas.

V$SHARED_POOL_RESERVED

Contains statistics about the SHARED_POOL area of the SGA.

FREE_SPACE	NUMBER
AVG_FREE_SIZE	NUMBER
FREE_COUNT	NUMBER
MAX_FREE_SIZE	NUMBER
USED_SPACE	NUMBER
AVG_USED_SIZE	NUMBER
USED_COUNT	NUMBER
MAX_USED_SIZE	NUMBER
REQUESTS	NUMBER
REQUEST_MISSES	NUMBER
LAST_MISS_SIZE	NUMBER
MAX_MISS_SIZE	NUMBER
REQUEST_FAILURES	NUMBER
LAST_FAILURE_SIZE	NUMBER
ABORTED_REQUEST_THRESHOLD	NUMBER
ABORTED_REQUESTS	NUMBER
LAST_ABORTED_SIZE	NUMBER

NOTE

If the initialization parameter SHARED_POOL_RESERVED_ SIZE has not been set, then only the following columns will be meaningful: REQUEST_FAILURES, LAST_FAILURE_SIZE, ABORTED_REQUEST_THRESHOLD, ABORTED_REQUESTS, and LAST_ABORTED_FILE.

V$VPD_POLICY

Lists all of the security policies and predicates associated with the cursors that are currently in the library cache.

ADDRESS	RAW(4)
PARADDR	RAW(4)
SQL_HASH	NUMBER
CHILD_NUMBER	NUMBER
OBJECT_OWNER	VARCHAR2(30)
OBJECT_NAME	VARCHAR2(30)
POLICY_GROUP	VARCHAR2(30)
POLICY	VARCHAR2(30)
POLICY_FUNCTION_OWNER	VARCHAR2(30)
PREDICATE	VARCHAR2(4000)

NOTE

Virtual Private Databases (VPDs) can be used to implement completely separate logical databases in the same Oracle database using fine-grained security policies.

SQL

The following views provide information about the processing of all SQL statements in the instance:

V$OBJECT_DEPENDENCY

Lists all objects that a package, procedure, or cursor in the SGA is depending on.

FROM_ADDRESS	RAW(4)
FROM_HASH	NUMBER
TO_OWNER	VARCHAR2(64)
TO_NAME	VARCHAR2(1000)
TO_ADDRESS	RAW(4)
TO_HASH	NUMBER
TO_TYPE	NUMBER

NOTE

You can join the V$OBJECT_DEPENDENCY view to the V$SQL and V$SESSION views to obtain a list of all objects being referenced by a user.

V$OPEN_CURSOR

Lists all open cursors in the system.

SADDR	RAW(4)
SID	NUMBER
USER_NAME	VARCHAR2(30)
ADDRESS	RAW(4)
HASH_VALUE	NUMBER
SQL_TEXT	VARCHAR2(60)

V$SORT_SEGMENT

Provides information about all sort segments in tablespaces specified as TEMPORARY.

TABLESPACE_NAME	VARCHAR2(31)
SEGMENT_FILE	NUMBER
SEGMENT_BLOCK	NUMBER
EXTENT_SIZE	NUMBER
CURRENT_USERS	NUMBER
TOTAL_EXTENTS	NUMBER
TOTAL_BLOCKS	NUMBER
USED_EXTENTS	NUMBER
USED_BLOCKS	NUMBER
FREE_EXTENTS	NUMBER
FREE_BLOCKS	NUMBER
ADDED_EXTENTS	NUMBER
EXTENT_HITS	NUMBER
FREED_EXTENTS	NUMBER
FREE_REQUESTS	NUMBER
MAX_SIZE	NUMBER
MAX_BLOCKS	NUMBER
MAX_USED_SIZE	NUMBER
MAX_USED_BLOCKS	NUMBER
MAX_SORT_SIZE	NUMBER
MAX_SORT_BLOCKS	NUMBER
RELATIVE_FNO	NUMBER

V$SORT_USAGE

Provides information about sort segments in all tablespaces.

TABLESPACE_NAME	VARCHAR2(31)
SEGMENT_FILE	NUMBER
SEGMENT_BLOCK	NUMBER
EXTENT_SIZE	NUMBER
CURRENT_USERS	NUMBER
TOTAL_EXTENTS	NUMBER
TOTAL_BLOCKS	NUMBER
USED_EXTENTS	NUMBER
USED_BLOCKS	NUMBER
FREE_EXTENTS	NUMBER

FREE_BLOCKS	NUMBER
ADDED_EXTENTS	NUMBER
EXTENT_HITS	NUMBER
FREED_EXTENTS	NUMBER
FREE_REQUESTS	NUMBER
MAX_SIZE	NUMBER
MAX_BLOCKS	NUMBER
MAX_USED_SIZE	NUMBER
MAX_USED_BLOCKS	NUMBER
MAX_SORT_SIZE	NUMBER
MAX_SORT_BLOCKS	NUMBER
RELATIVE_FNO	NUMBER

V$SQL

Provides information about all SQL statements in the shared SQL area.

SQL_TEXT	VARCHAR2(1000)
SHARABLE_MEM	NUMBER
PERSISTENT_MFM	NUMBER
RUNTIME_MEM	NUMBER
SORTS	NUMBER
LOADED_VERSIONS	NUMBER
OPEN_VERSIONS	NUMBER
USERS_OPENING	NUMBER
FETCHES	NUMBER
EXECUTIONS	NUMBER
USERS_EXECUTING	NUMBER
LOADS	NUMBER
FIRST_LOAD_TIME	VARCHAR2(19)
INVALIDATIONS	NUMBER
PARSE_CALLS	NUMBER
DISK_READS	NUMBER
BUFFER_GETS	NUMBER
ROWS_PROCESSED	NUMBER
COMMAND_TYPE	NUMBER
OPTIMIZER_MODE	VARCHAR2(10)
OPTIMIZER_COST	NUMBER
PARSING_USER_ID	NUMBER
PARSING_SCHEMA_ID	NUMBER
KEPT_VERSIONS	NUMBER
ADDRESS	RAW(4)
TYPE_CHK_HEAP	RAW(4)
HASH_VALUE	NUMBER
PLAN_HASH_VALUE	NUMBER
CHILD_NUMBER	NUMBER
MODULE	VARCHAR2(64)
MODULE_HASH	NUMBER
ACTION	VARCHAR2(64)

ACTION_HASH	NUMBER
SERIALIZABLE_ABORTS	NUMBER
OUTLINE_CATEGORY	VARCHAR2(64)
CPU_TIME	NUMBER
ELAPSED_TIME	NUMBER
OUTLINE_SID	NUMBER
CHILD_ADDRESS	RAW(4)
SQLTYPE	NUMBER
REMOTE	VARCHAR2(1)
OBJECT_STATUS	VARCHAR2(19)
LITERAL_HASH_VALUE	NUMBER
LAST_LOAD_TIME	VARCHAR2(19)
IS_OBSOLETE	VARCHAR2(1)
CHILD_LATCH	NUMBER

V$SQL_BIND_DATA

Provides information about bind variables in each SQL statement.

SQL_TEXT	VARCHAR2(1000)
SHARABLE_MEM	NUMBER
PERSISTENT_MEM	NUMBER
RUNTIME_MEM	NUMBER
SORTS	NUMBER
LOADED_VERSIONS	NUMBER
OPEN_VERSIONS	NUMBER
USERS_OPENING	NUMBER
FETCHES	NUMBER
EXECUTIONS	NUMBER
USERS_EXECUTING	NUMBER
LOADS	NUMBER
FIRST_LOAD_TIME	VARCHAR2(19)
INVALIDATIONS	NUMBER
PARSE_CALLS	NUMBER
DISK_READS	NUMBER
BUFFER_GETS	NUMBER
ROWS_PROCESSED	NUMBER
COMMAND_TYPE	NUMBER
OPTIMIZER_MODE	VARCHAR2(10)
OPTIMIZER_COST	NUMBER
PARSING_USER_ID	NUMBER
PARSING_SCHEMA_ID	NUMBER
KEPT_VERSIONS	NUMBER
ADDRESS	RAW(4)
TYPE_CHK_HEAP	RAW(4)
HASH_VALUE	NUMBER
PLAN_HASH_VALUE	NUMBER
CHILD_NUMBER	NUMBER
MODULE	VARCHAR2(64)

MODULE_HASH	NUMBER
ACTION	VARCHAR2(64)
ACTION_HASH	NUMBER
SERIALIZABLE_ABORTS	NUMBER
OUTLINE_CATEGORY	VARCHAR2(64)
CPU_TIME	NUMBER
ELAPSED_TIME	NUMBER
OUTLINE_SID	NUMBER
CHILD_ADDRESS	RAW(4)
SQLTYPE	NUMBER
REMOTE	VARCHAR2(1)
OBJECT_STATUS	VARCHAR2(19)
LITERAL_HASH_VALUE	NUMBER
LAST_LOAD_TIME	VARCHAR2(19)
IS_OBSOLETE	VARCHAR2(1)
CHILD_LATCH	NUMBER

V$SQL_BIND_METADATA

Provides metadata about all bind variables used in SQL statements.

ADDRESS	RAW(4)
POSITION	NUMBER
DATATYPE	NUMBER
MAX_LENGTH	NUMBER
ARRAY_LEN	NUMBER
BIND_NAME	VARCHAR2(30)

V$SQL_CURSOR

Provides debugging information about every cursor in the shared SQL area.

CURNO	NUMBER
FLAG	NUMBER
STATUS	VARCHAR2(9)
PARENT_HANDLE	RAW(4)
PARENT_LOCK	RAW(4)
CHILD_LOCK	RAW(4)
CHILD_PIN	RAW(4)
PERS_HEAP_MEM	NUMBER
WORK_HEAP_MEM	NUMBER
BIND_VARS	NUMBER
DEFINE_VARS	NUMBER
BIND_MEM_LOC	VARCHAR2(64)
INST_FLAG	VARCHAR2(64)
INST_FLAG2	VARCHAR2(64)

V$SQL_PLAN

Shows the plan used to execute recent SQL statements. New
with Oracle9*i*.

ADDRESS	RAW(4)
HASH_VALUE	NUMBER
CHILD_NUMBER	NUMBER
OPERATION	VARCHAR2(30)
OPTIONS	VARCHAR2(30)
OBJECT_NODE	VARCHAR2(10)
OBJECT#	NUMBER
OBJECT_OWNER	VARCHAR2(30)
OBJECT_NAME	VARCHAR2(64)
OPTIMIZER	VARCHAR2(20)
ID	NUMBER
PARENT_ID	NUMBER
DEPTH	NUMBER
POSITION	NUMBER
SEARCH_COLUMNS	NUMBER
COST	NUMBER
CARDINALITY	NUMBER
BYTES	NUMBER
OTHER_TAG	VARCHAR2(35)
PARTITION_START	VARCHAR2(5)
PARTITION_STOP	VARCHAR2(5)
PARTITION_ID	NUMBER
OTHER	VARCHAR2(4000)
DISTRIBUTION	VARCHAR2(20)
CPU_COST	NUMBER
IO_COST	NUMBER
TEMP_SPACE	NUMBER
ACCESS_PREDICATES	VARCHAR2(4000)
FILTER_PREDICATES	VARCHAR2(4000)

NOTE

Information in the V$SQL_PLAN view is similar to the
information you would receive from using the EXPLAIN
PLAN command, except that this information is a log of
the plan actually used rather than a description of the
plan that will probably be used.

V$SQL_REDIRECTION

Lists the SQL statements that have been redirected, along
with the reason for the redirection, such as a query rewrite,

---

with materialized views or an invalid object that was referenced. New with Oracle9i.

ADDRESS	RAW(4)
PARENT_HANDLE	RAW(4)
HASH_VALUE	NUMBER
CHILD_NUMBER	NUMBER
PARSING_USER_ID	NUMBER
PARSING_SCHEMA_ID	NUMBER
COMMAND_TYPE	NUMBER
REASON	VARCHAR2(14)
ERROR_CODE	NUMBER
POSITION	NUMBER
SQL_TEXT_PIECE	VARCHAR2(1000)
ERROR_MESSAGE	VARCHAR2(1000)

V$SQL_SHARED_MEMORY

Provides information about how memory is allocated for
every cursor in the shared SQL area.

SQL_TEXT	VARCHAR2(1000)
HASH_VALUE	NUMBER
HEAP_DESC	RAW(4)
STRUCTURE	VARCHAR2(16)
FUNCTION	VARCHAR2(16)
CHUNK_COM	VARCHAR2(16)
CHUNK_PTR	RAW(4)
CHUNK_SIZE	NUMBER
ALLOC_CLASS	VARCHAR2(8)
CHUNK_TYPE	NUMBER
SUBHEAP_DESC	RAW(4)

V$SQL_WORKAREA

Provides information on resource usage for the work areas
used by SQL cursors. New with Oracle9i.

ADDRESS	RAW(4)
HASH_VALUE	NUMBER
CHILD_NUMBER	NUMBER
WORKAREA_ADDRESS	RAW(4)
OPERATION_TYPE	VARCHAR2(20)
OPERATION_ID	NUMBER
POLICY	VARCHAR2(10)
ESTIMATED_OPTIMAL_SIZE	NUMBER
ESTIMATED_ONEPASS_SIZE	NUMBER
LAST_MEMORY_USED	NUMBER
LAST_EXECUTION	VARCHAR2(10)
LAST_DEGREE	NUMBER
TOTAL_EXECUTIONS	NUMBER
OPTIMAL_EXECUTIONS	NUMBER

ONEPASS_EXECUTIONS	NUMBER
MULTIPASSES_EXECUTIONS	NUMBER
ACTIVE_TIME	NUMBER
MAX_TEMPSEG_SIZE	NUMBER
LAST_TEMPSEG_SIZE	NUMBER

V$SQL_WORKAREA_ACTIVE

Provides instantaneous information on the currently active work areas. New with Oracle9i.

WORKAREA_ADDRESS	RAW(4)
OPERATION_TYPE	VARCHAR2(20)
OPERATION_ID	NUMBER
POLICY	VARCHAR2(6)
SID	NUMBER
QCINST_ID	NUMBER
QCSID	NUMBER
ACTIVE_TIME	NUMBER
WORK_AREA_SIZE	NUMBER
EXPECTED_SIZE	NUMBER
ACTUAL_MEM_USED	NUMBER
MAX_MEM_USED	NUMBER
NUMBER_PASSES	NUMBER
TEMPSEG_SIZE	NUMBER
TABLESPACE	VARCHAR2(31)
SEGRFNO#	NUMBER
SEGBLK#	NUMBER

NOTE

You can join the V$SQL_WORKAREA_ACTIVE view with V$SQL_WORKAREA using the column WORKAREA_ADDRESS to access the definition of that work area.

V$SQLAREA

Provides information on all SQL statements in the shared SQL area. Available after database is opened.

SQL_TEXT	VARCHAR2(1000)
SHARABLE_MEM	NUMBER
PERSISTENT_MEM	NUMBER
RUNTIME_MEM	NUMBER
SORTS	NUMBER
VERSION_COUNT	NUMBER
LOADED_VERSIONS	NUMBER
OPEN_VERSIONS	NUMBER
USERS_OPENING	NUMBER

FETCHES	NUMBER
EXECUTIONS	NUMBER
USERS_EXECUTING	NUMBER
LOADS	NUMBER
FIRST_LOAD_TIME	VARCHAR2(19)
INVALIDATIONS	NUMBER
PARSE_CALLS	NUMBER
DISK_READS	NUMBER
BUFFER_GETS	NUMBER
ROWS_PROCESSED	NUMBER
COMMAND_TYPE	NUMBER
OPTIMIZER_MODE	VARCHAR2(25)
PARSING_USER_ID	NUMBER
PARSING_SCHEMA_ID	NUMBER
KEPT_VERSIONS	NUMBER
ADDRESS	RAW(4)
HASH_VALUE	NUMBER
MODULE	VARCHAR2(64)
MODULE_HASH	NUMBER
ACTION	VARCHAR2(64)
ACTION_HASH	NUMBER
SERIALIZABLE_ABORTS	NUMBER
CPU_TIME	NUMBER
ELAPSED_TIME	NUMBER
IS_OBSOLETE	VARCHAR2(1)
CHILD_LATCH	NUMBER

NOTE

The V$SQLAREA view provides statistics on SQL statements that are in memory, parsed, and ready for execution.

V$SQLTEXT

Provides the text of all SQL statements in the shared SQL area.

ADDRESS	RAW(4)
HASH_VALUE	NUMBER
COMMAND_TYPE	NUMBER
PIECE	NUMBER
SQL_TEXT	VARCHAR2(64)

V$SQLTEXT_WITH_NEWLINES

Provides the text of all SQL statements in the shared SQL area but includes the original newline and tab characters.

ADDRESS	RAW(4)
HASH_VALUE	NUMBER
COMMAND_TYPE	NUMBER
PIECE	NUMBER
SQL_TEXT	VARCHAR2(64)

SQL*Loader direct path

The following views provide information relevant to current SQL*Loader direct path operations:

V$LOADCSTAT

Provides statistics about the number of rows processed during current SQL*Loader direct path operations.

READ	NUMBER
REJECTED	NUMBER
TDISCARD	NUMBER
NDISCARD	NUMBER

V$LOADPSTAT

Used by SQL*Loader to track statistics for current SQL*Loader direct path operations.

OWNER	VARCHAR2(31)
TABNAME	VARCHAR2(31)
PARTNAME	VARCHAR2(31)
LOADED	NUMBER

V$LOADTSTAT

Provides additional statistics about the number of rows discarded during current SQL*Loader direct path operations.

LOADED	NUMBER
REJECTED	NUMBER
FAILWHEN	NUMBER
ALLNULL	NUMBER
LEFT2SKIP	NUMBER
PTNLOADED	NUMBER

System environment

The following views provide information about the current environment:

V$DB_PIPES

Provides information about database pipes currently defined in the database.

OWNERID	NUMBER
NAME	VARCHAR2(1000)
TYPE	VARCHAR2(7)
PIPE_SIZE	NUMBER

V$DBLINK

Provides information about all currently open database links.

DB_LINK	VARCHAR2(128)
OWNER_ID	NUMBER
LOGGED_ON	VARCHAR2(3)
HETEROGENEOUS	VARCHAR2(3)
PROTOCOL	VARCHAR2(6)
OPEN_CURSORS	NUMBER
IN_TRANSACTION	VARCHAR2(3)
UPDATE_SENT	VARCHAR2(3)
COMMIT_POINT_STRENGTH	NUMBER

V$FILESTAT

Provides information about the current read/write status of all data files.

FILE#	NUMBER
PHYRDS	NUMBER
PHYWRTS	NUMBER
PHYBLKRD	NUMBER
PHYBLKWRT	NUMBER
SINGLEBLKRDS	NUMBER
READTIM	NUMBER

WRITETIM	NUMBER
SINGLEBLKRDTIM	NUMBER
AVGIOTIM	NUMBER
LSTIOTIM	NUMBER
MINIOTIM	NUMBER
MAXIORTM	NUMBER
MAXIOWTM	NUMBER

V$FIXED_TABLE

Lists all V$ and X$ tables defined in the kernel.

NAME	VARCHAR2(30)
OBJECT_ID	NUMBER
TYPE	VARCHAR2(5)
TABLE_NUM	NUMBER

V$FIXED_VIEW_DEFINITION

Provides a view definition for each dynamic performance view based on the X$ tables.

| VIEW_NAME | VARCHAR2(30) |
| VIEW_DEFINITION | VARCHAR2(4000) |

NOTE

The V$FIXED_VIEW_DEFINITION view shows how each V$ view is related to the underlying X$ memory view.

V$GLOBAL_TRANSACTION

Provides information on all current global transactions.

FORMATID	NUMBER
GLOBALID	RAW(64)
BRANCHID	RAW(64)
BRANCHES	NUMBER
REFCOUNT	NUMBER
PREPARECOUNT	NUMBER
STATE	VARCHAR2(18)
FLAGS	NUMBER
COUPLING	VARCHAR2(15)

V$INDEXED_FIXED_COLUMN

Lists each index column in the tables listed in V$FIXED_TABLE.

TABLE_NAME	VARCHAR2(30)
INDEX_NUMBER	NUMBER
COLUMN_NAME	VARCHAR2(30)
COLUMN_POSITION	NUMBER

V$RESOURCE_LIMIT

Shows the current utilization of system resources that can be specified in the initialization file.

RESOURCE_NAME	VARCHAR2(30)
CURRENT_UTILIZATION	NUMBER
MAX_UTILIZATION	NUMBER
INITIAL_ALLOCATION	VARCHAR2(10)
LIMIT_VALUE	VARCHAR2(10)

V$ROLLNAME

Lists the names of all rollback segments defined in the database. Available after database is opened.

USN	NUMBER
NAME	#VARCHAR2(30)

V$ROLLSTAT

Provides statistics about each rollback segment.

USN	NUMBER
LATCH	NUMBER
EXTENTS	NUMBER
RSSIZE	NUMBER
WRITES	NUMBER
XACTS	NUMBER
GETS	NUMBER
WAITS	NUMBER
OPTSIZE	NUMBER
HWMSIZE	NUMBER
SHRINKS	NUMBER
WRAPS	NUMBER
EXTENDS	NUMBER
AVESHRINK	NUMBER
AVEACTIVE	NUMBER
STATUS	VARCHAR2(15)
CUREXT	NUMBER
CURBLK	NUMBER

V$SYSSTAT

Provides the current values for each of the system statistics defined in V$STATNAME.

STATISTIC#	NUMBER
NAME	VARCHAR2(64)
CLASS	NUMBER
VALUE	NUMBER

V$SYSTEM_CURSOR_CACHE

Provides information about cursor usage across all sessions.

OPENS	NUMBER
HITS	NUMBER
HIT_RATIO	NUMBER

V$SYSTEM_EVENT

Provides information about time spent waiting for each
system event defined in V$EVENT_NAME.

EVENT	VARCHAR2(64)
TOTAL_WAITS	NUMBER
TOTAL_TIMEOUTS	NUMBER
TIME_WAITED	NUMBER
AVERAGE_WAIT	NUMBER
TIME_WAITED_MICRO	NUMBER

V$TIMER

Provides access to a timer that increments every one-
hundredth of a second.

HSECS	NUMBER

V$TRANSACTION

Lists all active transactions in the system.

ADDR	RAW(4)
XIDUSN	NUMBER
XIDSLOT	NUMBER
XIDSQN	NUMBER
UBAFIL	NUMBER
UBABLK	NUMBER
UBASQN	NUMBER
UBAREC	NUMBER
STATUS	VARCHAR2(16)
START_TIME	VARCHAR2(20)
START_SCNB	NUMBER
START_SCNW	NUMBER
START_UEXT	NUMBER
START_UBAFIL	NUMBER
START_UBABLK	NUMBER
START_UBASQN	NUMBER

START_UBAREC	NUMBER
SES_ADDR	RAW(4)
FLAG	NUMBER
SPACE	VARCHAR2(3)
RECURSIVE	VARCHAR2(3)
NOUNDO	VARCHAR2(3)
PTX	VARCHAR2(3)
NAME	VARCHAR2(256)
PRV_XIDUSN	NUMBER
PRV_XIDSLT	NUMBER
PRV_XIDSQN	NUMBER
PTX_XIDUSN	NUMBER
PTX_XIDSLT	NUMBER
PTX_XIDSQN	NUMBER
DSCN-B	NUMBER
DSCN-W	NUMBER
USED_UBLK	NUMBER
USED_UREC	NUMBER
LOG_IO	NUMBER
PHY_IO	NUMBER
CR_GET	NUMBER
CR_CHANGE	NUMBER

V$TRANSACTION_ENQUEUE

Lists all enqueues held by active transactions in the system.

ADDR	RAW(4)
KADDR	RAW(4)
SID	NUMBER
TYPE	VARCHAR2(2)
ID1	NUMBER
ID2	NUMBER
LMODE	NUMBER
REQUEST	NUMBER
CTIME	NUMBER
BLOCK	NUMBER

V$WAITSTAT

Provides information about the number of waits and how long the system had to wait for each class of data block.

CLASS	VARCHAR2(18)
COUNT	NUMBER
TIME	NUMBER

Index

We'd like to hear your suggestions for improving our indexes. Send email to
index@oreilly.com.
